TOR & THE DEEP WEB 2 IN 1 PACK

LANCE HENDERSON

DARKNET

INTRODUCTION

"If you want total security, go to prison. There you're fed, clothed, given medical care and so on. The only thing lacking ... is freedom" - Dwight Eisenhower

Friend,

My name is Lance and I am the author of this book on encryption security and anonymity. I have been an encryption enthusiast as well as writing about security in general for over a decade. I have been a member of many security and encryption forums since the 1980s, and have been involved with computer technology long before that (yeah I know that makes me an old geezer). But if there is a security or encryption program out there, I have used it and experienced its strengths and its shortcomings and (more than likely) attracted the attention of the authorities (more on that later).

I was there when PGP first arrived on the scene and when Napster was the dominant method of p2p trading. I have used most versions of PGP, Drivecrypt, Bestcrypt, Truecrypt, Tor, Freenet, I2P and every spinoff and copycat you can think of.

Let's face it. Today we are constantly bombarded with news by the media of those trawled, raided, arrested, imprisoned, tortured and humiliated because they weren't necessarily breaking any law but because they did not know the difference between privacy and anonymity. I waited and waited for some smart hacker to put something up on Amazon to prevent this from happening.

Didn't happen.

So I decided it would be me. I stepped up to the plate pronto, though truth be told I had been meaning to put together some of the rudimentary elements of encryption security in such a way that a person without any knowledge of security encryption or anonymity could become familiar.

It is not a particularly advanced book, but rather a portal from which a beginner can step through with the assurance of anonymity when he is online. To that end I present a few tools (mostly free) at your disposal to accomplish this lofty goal. If you're an advanced user, you just might learn some hidden vulnerabilities in your favorite anonymity program.

A PhD in computer science is not required to use encryption. Neither are you required to be a programmer of any sort. You only have to know your way around your operating system and be able to follow directions to the letter. If you know how to install an operating system, or for that matter, any application at all, then you can safely use encryption programs to preserve your own digital data and safety.

PRIVACY AND ANONYMITY

If you're like one of the many billions of people on the planet who use the internet to surf the net, check email, download programs or do any kind of online work, then you probably know there are risks associated with being a habitual internet user. That's just how it is. But it is not *your* fault that there are so many latent traps and pitfalls associated with online spelunking, in whatever form that may be.

It is just a fact of life that the Good lives alongside the Evil in our lives, offline or online. This book is meant as a beginner's guide to distinguish between the Good and the Evil, and to conceal your online footprint. To be a ghost on the internet, that is our aim.

This book is not necessarily for the advanced, such as those who teach computer science courses, but rather it is for those who would like to learn to surf without compromising their identity, or having their online habits tracked 24/7, and who engage in some risky speech against their government once in a blue moon. It is also for those who might not know about some of the little known vulnerabilities in their favorite "anonymous" software programs. In the end, you just might learn there is a vast difference between "anonymity" and "privacy".

Let's start with the basics. I'll just put this out there so you know the weight of the privacy situation entirely. As of 2014, you are always being tracked on the internet in just about every way you can imagine. Search engines, cookie managers, download managers and everything you do online has the potential to make someone, somewhere, a LOT of money. Most of the time, this is because laser-targeted advertising is extremely profitable. The more they know about your habits, the more money they make.

How?

Simple. If they know more about your fears, your likes and dislikes, and how and where you spend your money, they can deliver targeted advertising to you. Laser targeted advertising. That means more power for them, less for you. Now, advertising in and of itself is not such a bad thing, but neither is a loaded gun sitting on top of the fridge. By itself it can do nothing. However it is the method of execution that defines its usefulness.

If you type any medical search term into a major search engine such as Google, Yahoo, or Bing, soon enough you'll start to see targeted ads. If you search for "how to cure a hangover", you might not see anything right away, since hangovers generally don't last that long. However if you were to type "how to cure herpes", you will likely be typing variations of that sentence over the course of a few weeks or months since it is not an easy condition to treat. Eventually you would see pay-per-click ads start to manifest themselves in your search engine results in the top corners. These ads might be selling all manner of snake-oil remedies for the cure to herpes, or they might be referrals to medical specialists.

The bottom line is this: why do they think you have this disease? The answer is because you repeatedly typed it into the search engine over the course of days/months. Over the course of a year, how much do you reveal about your medical history and identity to your favorite search engine? Do you ever wish you could keep this information private?

They like to "bubble" your identity based on how you search: the time between searches, the time of day, your country, your area. With the help of a very specific item in your internet portfolio called an IP address, they can even find out where you live, who your ISP is, and chart a course right to your very doorstep. With the help of Google Maps, and a whole plethora of other mapping applications, this can potentially lead to some very annoying and/or embarrassing situations. Do you think this information would be valuable to door-to-door salesmen? Or perhaps a company that sends out mailed advertisements? Of course.

But first things first, let's briefly say a word about the difference between privacy and anonymity since many would-be geeks confuse the two. They are not the same thing. Not by a long shot.

Anonymity & Privacy - The Differences

WHILE WE SHOULDN'T WASTE time splitting hairs here, it is probably a good idea to distinguish between the terms "privacy" and "anonymity". The two terms are not really as interchangeable as you think. Let's say that you have Firefox running, and you are working from home with a direct connection to your ISP. You don't want anyone knowing what you're doing, so you select the "private mode" tab in Firefox. This disables cookies and inhibits the ability to store any remembered websites (unless you choose to do so).

However this privacy only goes so far. It does nothing for the IP address problem we discussed earlier. Search engines still see it, as does your internet service provider. Both entities know which sites you visit and for how long, based on your IP address. In short, they can see everything. Your wife can't, however. That is why the privacy mode in web browsers were built: to keep the sites you visit private and out of the public view.

Is this privacy enough for your needs? You certainly have some level of privacy, but anonymity is another matter. Anonymity takes privacy to an entirely different level, where the IP address, and thus anything you do online, is extinguished like a wet cloth to a candle's flame through layer after layer of digital barriers. If you want to have privacy, use Firefox's private mode, or use a VPN service provider in conjunction with this feature to ensure no one else in your household can see your online footprints. This assumes that they do not have access to your laptop or PC.

If that's the case, it's game over.

If on the other hand you want anonymity, there are several tools are your disposal, one of which is to use the Tor network. In doing so, you will guarantee yourself strict anonymity and be assured of simple privacy as well, provided you don't do something stupid like blurt out enough info (on a forum, for instance) that narrows you down to a city or state.

THE ANONYMOUS TOR NETWORK

"If money is your hope for independence you will never have it. The only real security that a man will have in this world is a reserve of knowledge, experience, and ability."
  Henry Ford

Every Internet Service Provider assigns an IP address to every user who logs into their network. From there, you can connect to the millions of websites, newsgroups, and online applications that you enjoy most. IP addresses are like phone numbers. They tell your computer where to connect and send packets of data. They need this information to not only send data, such as html code, but also flash code so you can watch Youtube videos. These are targeted with ads, too. And if you bring up task manager in Windows, you can see Flash player running. Do you think Adobe is not sending data back to them about your habits? Let's continue.

So, if the security of online privacy involves concealing the IP address between two computers, how do those two computers talk to each other without a direct connection? If you hide the phone number, how do you make the call? The answer is simple: you have someone else in another country dial the number for you. This is the first step to being anonymous online. Do not use the IP address (yours) as a direct connection. Hire a middle man to do the talking for you. How is this possible? There are several ways. You can use the free online program called Tor, which acts a relay point between you and your online destination. There are also paid services called VPNs (virtual private networks) as well as other anonymous networks like Freenet and I2P, but we'll get into the specifics of those later.

First and foremost, let's talk about Tor.

It is the quintessential solution to online privacy since it masks your IP address. The websites you connect to have no way of knowing where you live, which ISP you are using, or what your browsing habits are. When you connect to the Tor network, you are establishing a conduit whereby if you connect to a website (Google for instance), it connects through several layers of IP addresses, or "onion layers" to reach its destination. You send out a message, email, or some type of communication. The message then goes to Bob, Jane and Herb, then finally reaches the end of the line...your favorite webpage. It routes data (backwards/forwards) through an onion later of IP addresses, so that no one adversary can see who sent what without very significant resources.

As you have probably guessed, there is a small speed hit in doing this. In order to hide your IP address, several "hops" or intermediaries, have to be jumped through. Like portals. Without going into too much technical detail, let's just say that these hops serve a very valuable purpose: to keep your private communications out of the hands of those that intend to snoop on you. Since your IP address changes every time you login to the Tor network, they can't "bubble" you effectively and target you with ads because you look like a different person from a foreign country to them each time you login. The Tor relay will end up giving you a different country to "pop-out" from with each session of your Tor browser, thus making it impossible to know your origin or where you will go next.

Let's examine an analogy between Tor and regular internet usage. You're sitting in your living room browsing anonymously via the Tor network. Your wife on the other hand is sitting in the kitchen on her Macbook, browsing without Tor. You might wonder if her browsing habits break your own anonymity. They don't...up to a point. While your isp doesn't know what *you* are doing online, they certainly do in regards to your wife.

Imagine yourself driving down Main Street in a Mercedes with tinted windows. No one can peer inside to see what you are doing at the stoplight. Not even the cops. Your wife on the other hand has non-tinted windows. People can glance over without any effort and tell if she is smoking a cigarette, listening to her iPod or talking on her phone. You are anonymous. She is not. The ISP along with any websites she visits can see everything she does online. They can't see what you are doing, however.

Firefox (and many other browsers) talk to different hosts, with the router acting as the traffic cop. An example:

Your machine: Port X, Machine A (Tor: all encrypted traffic)
    Your wife: Port Y, Machine B (without Tor: all visible traffic)

It's like shooting fish in a barrel, and for the NSA, even easier than that. This same concept also applies with other things you may do on your machine while using Tor. If you use BitTorrent, your ISP can still see what you do on the P2P network even if you are running Tor simultaneously. But it cannot see the contents of the Tor network.

Thus, don't do anything on your P2P network that you wouldn't want your ISP to know about. Tor however is a different story since they cannot see what is going on between Tor relays. For all intents and purposes, Tor is like a cloak of invisibility that shields you from the sight of all onlookers, unless you have accidentally ripped a hole in the cloak (i.e. turned on javascript). If you are thinking, "Wow, it might be cool to run BitTorrent through Tor so I won't get sued". A nice goal, except BitTorrent devs aren't falling over themselves to implement this feature with Tor, and the Tor network can't really handle the bandwidth anyway. You'll just make everyone else miserable by downloading those 720p Blu-Ray rips you can easily get from Usenet (and with SSL, you're not likely to get sued.)

It might be prudent to spell out some of the best practices of using the Tor network should you decide to use it. First, although the Tor package comes with a preconfigured Firefox browser, there are still some rules you should follow that might not be apparent.

- Never give any compromising information on the Tor network that could be used to identify you. This means using your credit card for purchases, accessing your bank account, or logging into a social media site like Facebook. Card transaction are traceable. Tor, in fact, may even result in flagging transactions done via a tor exit node.
- Never mix browsers. Don't use the same browser you browse every day to Facebook and your ISP email as you do to access the Tor network. Super cookies can give away which sites you visit outside of Tor and can lead to a correlation attack on your identity/IP address.
- Always disable Javascript. The reason for this is that exploits can be utilized to reveal your IP address through using flash. Flash videos such as those on Youtube only work if this is enabled. After installation of Tor, ensure that the settings in the NoScript plugin are ON and not off by default in the plugins options screen.
- Install a bare minimum of browser plugins. You want to be as vanilla as everyone else. Too many addins, plugins, games, etc., can act as an identity beacon--fonts you use,

time of day you use certain features, can all be used to build a profile on you. BE VANILLA.

- Disable any automatic updates in the browser's options tab. This also includes updates for any addons. You should update manually, not automatically.

TOR AND TORRENTS

A word about torrents and the Tor network. It might seem on the surface that running your torrent client through the Tor network would be an obviously beneficial idea. After all, if Tor can cloak your regular Firefox downloads, surely it can do the same with torrents too, right? Well, yes and no. Yes, you could route your traffic through Tor using your favorite torrent client, however this is not a good idea for several reasons.

The first is that Tor was never developed to withstand the kind of punishing traffic bandwidth that usually comes from torrenting.

Secondly, most torrent clients like uTorrent, BitSpirit, and libTorrent are not coded properly to make you anonymous on the Tor network. They often will ignore their socks proxy settings since UDP protocol is heavily involved with torrenting, and will send your real IP address to the tracker, thereby defeating the purpose of using Tor completely. Tor in fact still does what it is coded to do: send whatever packets anonymously through the Tor network to your destination. However, it sends your IP address within the torrent tracker right along with it...anonymously.

It would be like sending a secret message in an envelope directly to the person you are attempting to hide that message from. This is not a problem with the Tor application, but rather the way torrent trackers are coded. The only fix would be if the torrent application coders themselves rewrote their applications to work harmoniously with the Tor network, something they probably will not get around to doing anytime soon (and much to the glee of Tor developers).

Tor Onion Sites

ONE OF THE most secretive elements of the Tor network is the existence of Tor Onion websites, which are pseudo top level domains acting as anonymous hidden services. In other words, they are hidden in that they can only be accessed by the Tor users themselves residing within the Tor network, rather from the open web. The motive for the creation of such hidden sites is so that the admin of the site as well as those accessing such sites cannot be traced. Since onion sites that are based on the hidden service protocol cannot be accessed from the regular internet, the address of the onion site you are looking for must be known. You can connect to an onion website on Tor just as you can a regular website, by typing the address into the address bar. For example, you might want to go to Tor2Web, in which case the address is:

http://tor2web.org/

A warning about tor2web: it is intended to offer one-sided security, that is, to protect the identity of those publishing content on Tor, not those browsing it. If you want to be secure while browsing you'll need to install the Tor application. Convenience and speed should always take a back seat where security is concerned.

Needless to say, a hidden network would not stay completely benign of nefarious webmasters if it wasn't indeed anonymous. To that end, the Hidden Wiki was developed, a singular .onion page with a wikipedia-like structure outlining in explicit detail everything from political activists to every conceivable criminal group imaginable. There are links to hundreds of various .onion sites dealing with everything from how to obtain illegal drugs, warez operations, virus creation, anonymous use of Bitcoins, illegal pornography, hacked Paypal accounts and even how to hire contract killers. Needless to say, some of these sites need to be taken with a grain of salt.

Be aware of your own country's laws regarding what can legally be obtained. What goes around in Amsterdam or Japan may not fly straight with the authorities in the USA. Remember that information that exists in Deep Web is just that: information. By itself, the information can do nothing. Words are just rearranged letters to get your point across. Pictures and videos are simply ones and zeros moving across your display. It is what they are eventually used for that define their ethics.

At the core of it, the Hidden Wiki is not terribly dissimilar from any run-of-the-mill black market operation offline. It just so happens to be online, and accessible by anyone with a little search engine sleuthing capability. Not all of the information in the Deep Web is used for nefarious purposes. Like Freenet, there are a lot of different sites that concentrate on exposing human rights abuse, political corruption, and government scandals involving high-level politicians. In the end, it is what you do with the data that determines the criminal element.

Testing your IP address visibility on Tor

WHEN YOU HAVE INSTALLED TOR, you may want to test your IP address to see if it really is broadcasting your Tor IP and not your real IP address. If you installed the default package of Tor, then Tor will show you the IP you are broadcasting as your start page. If you want to check it yourself, then go to

http://whatismyipaddress.com/.

This will show you not only your IP address, but your internet service provider as well, and where it is located on google maps. It will also show city and country. When you are using Tor, you will see a different city/country than the one you currently reside in. Mark down what your IP address is outside of Tor, and check this site when your launch Tor if you're especially paranoid (I am).

VPNS

The last few years have seen an emergence of many different VPN (virtual private network) providers with server farms in just about every country. What a VPN does is somewhat similar to what the Tor network does. It sends a different IP address to your destination, whether that is a webpage, usenet provider, or webhost. There are some pros and cons to this. First, it is not free. A VPN will cost the same amount you would get for Usenet service: about ten dollars per month. This amount fluctuates from provider to provider. Sometimes it is a little more, sometimes a bit less, but all providers have you login to their service the same way you would an ISP. Most of the configuration is automatic and doesn't require any technical wizardry to setup. Five minutes, give or take.

Another major difference is that while Tor provides anonymity, and is free, a VPN will provide you with *privacy*, but not necessarily *anonymity*. This is because the middle man, the VPN in this case, knows your real IP address. They have to know this information in order to forward your requests. The VPN service is built upon a different technology than Tor. It is built for *speed* and *stability*. Torrenting, you say? Knock yourself out.

Further, let's say that you're a Chinese dissident. You don't like the way your country is headed in regards to free speech and human rights. You can't exactly criticize the Chinese government in the Saturday paper can you? Of course not. So what is a good, law-abiding dissident to do? You build a news website using a VPN in another country and relay your dissent through that internet portal. You don't necessarily have to build a website. You could simply setup your newsreader to access Usenet via the VPN connection. In that way, the Chinese government could not determine the origin of any anti-governmental messages through the use of the IP address (unless of course you hint of incriminating personal information that narrows down your location).

You can also access forbidden places by the Chinese government, such as Facebook, Skype, private chat rooms and even Usenet. The reason these kinds of places are blocked by the Great Firewall of China is precisely because they are fertile ground for free speech enthusiasts. While this may sound like an easy way to circumvent the Chinese police, remember that most VPN providers offer connections through almost every civilized country you can think of. If you are a Chinese dissident, I wouldn't connect to a VPN located in China, but rather Canada or perhaps a country hostile to China. Most VPN providers offer a selection of many servers to choose from in which to route your messages and traffic.

On that note, let's talk a bit about law enforcement and VPNs. Many in the past have erroneously thought that a VPN carried with it a strong dose of anonymity, similar to what Tor offered. It doesn't quite stack up that way. A VPN service offers privacy, not anonymity, as we stated. They do not route your data through intermediaries the way Tor does. Depending on which VPN you choose, you could end up with one in Switzerland who will not cave to anyone's request for subscriber information outside of Sweden. On the other hand, you might have a US based provider who will bow down to the whims of any judge's warrant for subscriber information in a New York minute.

While most are perfectly safe for purposes of torrents and the like, one should think twice about using a VPN in a western country for felonious offenses, as they will most likely give your name and address up to law enforcement in order to stave off any fines and/or trouble by the government. There are of course ways around this, such as not using your credit card and paying anonymously, however sometimes it is better not to use a VPN at all for those kinds of purposes (think hackers, smuggling, illicit banned goods, drugs etc). Vpns have never been built with anonymity in mind. Tread carefully.

TOR RELAYS

"Who can you trust? Nobody, cause nobody wants you here."

Those words, uttered by Sean Connery in The Untouchables, are as appropriate for darknet discussions as they are for the mob. But let's be realistic for a moment. There are, as you read this, ten thousand more organized crime syndicates spread out over the net than you will ever come across in the "Deep Web". They run the same secure, enterprise-grade software that Wall Street banks use and cloak themselves better than Ringwraiths. No outside eyes peer in unless the alphabet agency has a guy on the inside. Cartels like these rake in millions in drugs, arms, counterfeit pharmaceuticals, mercs and excel at human trafficking.

The Deep Web is similar, but not that similar. But those who are for outlawing it completely are really advocating for more control rather than for less crime, as was the case with Prohibition. They claim the negatives outweigh the positives. Let's say a guy in North Korea gets curious as to why his government is censoring information from him. He wants to know why. So he uses Tor to access websites blocked by the North Korean regime (Facebook for instance, to hook up with an uncle who may have escaped to S. Korea). And he does so anonymously. So that is one positive trait.

But this, they say, does not outweigh the child porn, contract killers and heroin runners. They say, people aren't going to Tor to discuss ways of avoiding the mine fields on the border and neither are they discussing the latest enlightenment from Tibet. Yes, anonymity has its meritorious moments, but someone who wants to hide almost always does so at the circumvention of the law. There are only so many North Koreans, after all.

They assume, quite wrongly, that those criminals engaged in the above activities would cease to exist. They are wrong. These were around before Tor and the Deep Web were even a spark in the developer's minds, and will thrive regardless of what government regulations are cooked up by congress critters. The same as it was during Prohibition.

Hazards of running a Tor Exit Node

In 2012, an Austrian named William Weber, an IT admin, was arrested for running Tor servers that route anonymous traffic over the Tor network. The charge? Distributing illegal images. Police detected the data coming off one of the nodes he ran. A police raid ensued. Searched his home. Confiscated his Xbox, iPods, all drives and miscellaneous electronics and even his legally owned firearms. The court order revealed one of the Tor exit nodes (he ran seven) was transporting the data.

Notice, we did not state that *he* transported the data. The data in question is going to come down on some node, be it his or someone else's. That is how Tor works: via encrypted traffic that gets piped through servers on its own IP address, through various layers (hence the term Onion layer) and decrypted back into its initial form. An ISP cannot discern the contents in transit. However, law enforcement can see the contents coming out of a node that was sent from the other side of the globe. Holding a Tor node operator responsible would be like holding a forum administrator responsible because some anonymous poster said he was going to kill the president.

Misuse of Tor end nodes are fairly common. Back in 2008, a man was arrested by German police after bomb threats passed through his Tor node, and similarly, they confiscated all electronics--hardware, software, and threatened imprisonment because someone abused his generosity. These kinds of cases bring up a few parallels. Should the Austrian government sue Google for having illegal data flowing through its servers? We're not only talking about images or bomb threats. Warez, kidnapping, extortion, bribery, espionage, a long laundry list of crimes occur on a daily basis via their search engine, and though Google cooperates with law enforcement (as Weber did), when was the last time you heard Google's servers confiscated by a court order?

And then there is encryption. Should Drivecrypt and Truecrypt developers be held liable for helping illegal enterprises? Truecrypt is a software used quite heavily by Mexican cartels as well as organized crime in the United States. Law enforcement, particularly the FBI, tends to shoot first and ask questions later. Maybe. If they're in a good mood (or ordered to by a judge). Meanwhile, your electronics are confiscated and your reputation damaged.

The entire ordeal has been setting dangerous precedent for years, as any average Joe who just happens to pass some part of an illegal data packet through his connection (or unsecured WiFi) can be prosecuted. Furthermore, police are not known for their technical aptitude, in Austria or anywhere else. They took his Xbox360 and anything else plugged in that looked about as complex as a toaster. We mustn't allow Tor node operators to be scapegoats. If Tor dies, innocent people die. They won't get the word out about corrupt government actions without risking their own lives. And they shouldn't *have* to risk anything to get the word out.

As of 2014, no one has been sued or prosecuted in a U.S. court of law for running a Tor relay (unlike those using BitTorrent). Furthermore, using Tor as well as running a Tor relay is perfectly legal under U.S. law.

Benefits of Running a Tor Exit Node

We've talked a little about the risks of being a Tor exit mode. You might be saying, well, the risks far outweigh the benefits. And in some places, you're right. But it depends on where you live, the laws, the bandwidth, your setup, etc.

So what are the benefits?

- Help people all over the world browse the net anonymously (esp. censorship-prone countries)

- Provide support for the network

- Exit nodes are always scarce. Your generosity supports development.

- Defeat tyranny (what's that? Well, North Korea for one)

- Prevent websites/search engines from tracking you

- Help others get beyond the Great Firewall of China

- Join the Rebel Alliance (yeah right)

At this point it might be prudent to relay my own experience. The first time I used Tor, I was already fairly good as not only admin of several websites and hosted machines, but quite good at encryption. My frame of thought was, if I was no slouch at encryption, Tor would be a piece of cake. And it was...for a while. I had plenty of bandwidth available, so I jumped right in.

Being in North America at the time, it would be a few weeks to get up to speed on all the pros and cons of Tor relays, and not from the technical standpoint, but the legal. I envisioned Blackhawk helicopters and car chases involving white vans with license plates that read "NOTOJ" should I be so unlucky to screw up my configuration. Putting my paranoia aside, I finally got it running full speed, and studied the network logs like a hawk to see what it was doing. And I was well-pleased. Full of pride, you might say.

Tor traffic trickled in like a sprinkle before a storm, and after three days my node had spread just as the bandwidth limits I had preset kicked in. The feeling was euphoric. Addicting. I envisioned some tech-starved villager in North Korea accessing something verboten by the Korean government. I kept thinking about Matthew Broderick in WarGames and the famous line, "The only way to win the game, was not to play." Well, I tweaked it to add, "...by the Man's rules." It was all good.

Until a week later when my ISP ordered me to cut the Tor umbilical. It was polite, but stern. It seemed a few complaints sailed their way. As my luck would have it, that North Korean villager turned out to be a swarm of torrentors using Tor to evade the trackers setup by the record industry. It hampered Tor's bandwidth like a hurricane had set upon it.

"Torrents?" I said. "Really?"

Yes indeed. And even though I lived in Canada at the time and wasn't worried about a torrent of lawsuits, I still did not want other Tor users to be hindered by greedy users. The problem I ran into was that filtering torrent traffic is a bit counterproductive since BitTorrent is able to run on any standard port. I tried blocking ports 80 and 443 (web traffic). It wasn't a silver bullet, however, since torrent users could still use other ports. BitTorrent clients like uTorrent and BitLord can run on any port, almost all randomly chosen. Thus every port you add to your exit node can connect to another client listening on that same port. Some users even enable a range of ports, thereby increasing the chance of getting a DMCA takedown for you.

Hence, we come to the Reduced Exit Policy of Tor, an alternative to the default exit policy. You are still able to connect and at the same time block TCP ports (usually) used by BitTorrent users. Below are a couple of port lists to check against BitTorrent clients:

https://secure.wikimedia.org/wikipedia/en/wiki/List_of_TCP_and_
UDP_port_numbers

http://www.speedguide.net/ports.php

What should become clear as crystal at this point is that you should not run an exit relay from your house, with emphasis on *should not*. Why not? Because of the aforementioned scenarios with law enforcement. As we've seen in prior cases, it is quite easy for them to get a judge's signature (a judge who knows squat about Tor) on a no-knock warrant in the USA should they start sniffing your traffic. Not only will they take your computer, but everything with connectivity, which these days includes TVs and monitors. Much better to run the exit relay from a commercial provider (and there are many). A few in the U.S. who are not only knowledgeable about Tor, but have the support needed to deal with abuse cases are as follows:

Amazon Web Services (AWS)
    AmeriNOC
    Arvixe
    Axigy
    ChunkHost
    Team Cinipac
    Cyberonic
    Ethr.net
    Evolucix
    Future Hosting

A full comprehensive list is available at the Tor Wiki that covers many countries, each with their own subset of laws dealing with anonymity services (and extensive comments on each).

https://trac.torproject.org/projects/tor/wiki/doc/GoodBadISPs

In the event you do decide to run a Tor relay from home however, make sure you inform your ISP and ascertain whether you have their full support (i.e. no surprises a month down the line). The abuse complaints will come sooner or later, just as they did for me. The Tor forums have a list of ISPs that are friendly towards Tor and are knowledgeable about the network, in addition to ones that are not.

FREENET

Freenet is unlike any other anonymizing beast on the entire internet. It takes quite a wizardly mind to crack its protection and to that, it is a bit like chess: easy to grasp the basics, long and difficult to become a master. Built in 2000, Freenet is a vast, encrypted datastore spanning thousands of connected computers across the globe, all distributing encrypted contents from one computer to another. To this end, it is somewhat similar to a P2P program like Emule. Except with eEule, every file, whether it mp3, rar or iso is out there in the open for weeks, months and years, along with the IP addresses, trumpeting who downloaded and uploaded every file. You know what you upload, and what you download, and so does everyone else.

Freenet is different in this regard.

While your IP address is visible, what you are uploading out of your datastore is not. You initially setup the size of the datastore for others to download from you. This datastore is encrypted. You have no idea what will eventually be inside, as the contents are encrypted. It is a bit like a postal worker delivering the mail. He has no idea what is in the package he is delivering. That is not his job. His job is to deliver the contents to its destination. Therein is the strength of Freenet.

While you can see your downloads merrily trickle their way down to your laptop, there is no way to decrypt your datastore's content and see what it is you're passing along to the nearest node. And to that, the bigger the datastore, the more efficiently Freenet runs. After one inserts a file into Freenet, the user is free to shutdown their pc. This is unlike torrents in that the stability of the torrent file is dependent on the length of online seeds. Thus, high reliability is a factor with Freenet files, as the file is spread between encrypted blocks residing in the Freenet system.

Freenet is slow. So slow in fact, that you may not see any measurable progress in download speed for a couple hours or so after install, and it may be a day before you can see extensive progress with old (unpopular) files. Don't get discouraged because of this. It will speed up gradually over time.

Now, with your IP address out there in the open, you might be tempted to think it is not very anonymous. Nothing could be further from the truth. Whatever you download is encrypted from one end of Freenet to the other, and decrypted on your PC. No one looking in from the outside can see who requested which file or message. No one on the inside knows either, except you. For this reason alone, it is extremely censorship-resistant. This level of anonymity requires each node that requests data to operate in "hops", from many intermediaries, similar to what you would see in Tor.

However, no node knows who requested which file, thus giving a high level of anonymity. This requirement carries a price in that downloads as well as uploads are initially extremely slow, especially for new data inserts.

Let's say you want to share an iso dvd image on this network. You fire up Frost (a front-end addon for Freenet), then hit insert, then select the file. Then depending on how big your file is, you could be waiting for a long time, say several hours, for the file to finish. If this file had been inserted three months prior, and was very popular, with dozens of users trying to fetch said file, then that file would download very fast. However this is not usually the case with new files since every kernel of data on Freenet operates faster if and only if it is a popular file.

There are two types of security protocols that Freenet offers: Darknet and Openet. For Openet, you connect to other users, called "strangers". There is nothing sinister about this, as this is what the Freenet developers envisioned that most beginners would use. The IP address of said strangers is visible, but the anonymity of Freenet isn't nested in the security of the IP address like Tor, but rather it is nested in the encryption methods of the distributed datastore.

The other security option, which you are given at installation, is Darknet, where you will connect to "friends" rather than "strangers". These will be Freenet users that you will have (presumably) previously exchanged node references, which are public security keys. With Darknet mode, it is assumed that you will have a higher level of trust, as your node reference is related to your online Freenet identity. Needless to say, this mode is not to be taken lightly. You really do have to TRUST those you add to this protocol. That is, the darknet protocol.

Within Freenet, there are no censors. Every kind of free speech is allowable and often encouraged. The very way in which Freenet is programmed makes it impossible to remove any message from the system by a censor. Individual users may opt to erase certain comments from the frost system, for instance, but this is only at the local level, on their machine, and not the Freenet network itself. Thus, no religious group for instance can force others in the network to conform to their belief and discussion system. No one on Freenet may deem information so offensive that it must be removed. Not even Freenet developers.

Needless to say, this has some negative consequences in that anyone may say anything to anyone at any time. Some Freesites on the Freenet network are plagued by spammers, identity thieves, terrorists, molesters, government anarchists and software pirates. The

Freenet developers have stated this is a necessary evil of sorts in allowing 100% free speech to reign free. It could be argued that one should not allow illicit digital goods to be exchanged between users just so people could speak freely, however one of the stated purposes of Freenet is to preserve such a system in the even of societal collapse or oppression.

While there are no rules to govern Freenet by in the sense of censoring unsightly posts, a few guidelines have been posted in scattered parts of Freenet that should probably be heeded:

1.) NEVER GIVE anyone on Freenet your node-reference, as this contains information that could be exploited to correlate your Freenet identity with your IP address.

2.) Same rule as Usenet: Don't give in to trolling activity. Trolling by its very nature flourishes with the more responses it receives. Ignore them.

3.) Never give out any personal info: your location, where you grew up, which restaurants you like most, what kinds of clothing stores you shop at, as these could zero-in on your location

4.) Take notice of different regionally spelled words (labor vs. labour, color vs. colour: these could reveal your home country).

5.) Never use any nickname that is the very same unique nickname you use for opennet forums. Use popular nicknames like Shadow, John, Peter and the like.

THE HIGHEST SECURITY setting can be a bit foreboding, but perhaps necessary in countries where criticizing the government could land you a lifetime in a work camp. It has an encrypted password option to encrypt Freenet usage. This setting is in the security configuration, along with a host of other options of varying system requirements. The higher the security setting, the slower Freenet will run as it will use more resources to cover your footsteps.

When first installing Freenet, it will likely take no more than a few minutes, while asking you which security level you would like to operate at (normal up to maximum). After that and a bit of time allowed for Freenet to find nodes to connect to, you'll be presented with a previously hidden world where a Freenet index lists every possible combination of Freesites available. Everything from anarchy sites to Iranian news, to pirated copies of books, films and game roms and even a few political how to documents describing how to protest a corrupt government without getting caught will be indexed.

These are the types of things typically either censored by Google in China, or deindexed altogether. The only thing missing is a disclaimer at the bottom of the screen welcoming you to the deepest, darkest depths of the internet, known as Darknet.

Optionally, you may run Freenet from an encrypted Truecrypt container file. You will need to create a Truecrypt volume that is sufficiently large enough to hold whatever files you intend on downloading from Freenet. Remember to keep in mind that when Freenet asks you how large you want the datastore to be, the size you choose could be a benefit to other Freenet users. The larger the datastore, the more efficient the Freenet network operates.

That is not to say that downloads will *always* come down faster, but rather encrypted data will last longer on the network. This is similar to the retention times that Usenet providers talk about when they try to sell their servers to you. The higher the data retention, the longer the files on the network will last. There is also another bonus to having a large datastore, say fifty gigabytes or so. Files that you may request may already be in your datastore after having run Freenet for some time, thereby shortening the time to retrieve them.

With your Truecrypt container you can run Freenet with the volume mounted and not worry about your Freenet activities being used against you in case of your computer being confiscated. You can also do the same for your Tor browser as well. Install Tor browser bundle to a mounted Truecrypt container and only run the program when mounted.

Frost

FROST IS a separate application than Freenet, which acts as a front-end. It makes browsing on the Freenet network more akin to browsing Usenet newsgroups. Download at:

HTTP://JTCFROST.SOURCEFORGE.NET

AFTER RUNNING FREENET, you can optionally run Frost simultaneously to download inserts from the Freenet network. It is not mandatory but it is incredibly helpful. Run Freenet, then Frost, and then wait an hour or so for Frost to find some groups, and then hit the globe button at the top panel to subscribe to groups. These groups all have discussions going about every topic under the sun. Some of them are fairly dead, with almost no discussion at all, and others swarm with activity.

Frosty Tips

1.) If you started downloading something in Frost, finish it in Frost

2.) Like Usenet, don't troll the boards. It will get you put on user's "ignore" list and they will henceforth not see any messages from your nick.

3.) Never reveal your node reference to anyone on the Frost boards, as it could be used to locate you.

4.) Set days to download backwards to 60 (or however long you wish). Just be aware that it may take several days to retrieve all messages if you select a very large amount of days.

5.) In the options/preferences tab, you may adjust the setting to ignore comments from users with less than four messages attached to their nickname. This is very effective at eliminating most spam messages on the board.

TRUECRYPT, VERACRYPT, ETC.

There are two types of encryption: one that will prevent your sister from reading your diary and one that will prevent your government. - Bruce Schneier

IT WOULD BE FOLLY if we went to all this work of laying out the security options to keep our online footprint out of nefarious hands and not say something about our offline footprint. Put simply, you should tread carefully with your offline habits just as you should your online persona.

Let's say you're in your favorite cafe. You're sipping your ice cappuccino with your laptop in the corner of the coffee scented shop and have to make a break for the restroom. It'll only take a minute or so, right? While you're in there, the guy sitting at the next table decided to insert a USB key into your laptop and upload a keylogger virus into your machine. This keylogger is ridiculously small in size, and can hide undetected by most users. It can even disguise itself as a windows service and look just like any other svchost process, all the while taking snapshots of your screen, recording everything you typed for the remainder of that day, and emailing them to whomever installed the virus.

You would be a bit worried if you knew about it.

However, most don't realize they leave themselves vulnerable to such attacks in public places. Some experts have referred to this as the "evil maid attack", after a scenario whereby you are in a hotel and briefly step outside for a moment and at which point the maid comes in and has physical access to your running machine. They now have access to every cookie stored by your browser in addition to any credit card numbers you have used, possible phone numbers/emails of friends, and the like. How to prevent this?

For starters, to prevent identity theft you need to seriously consider full-disk encryption. This is not nearly as complex as you might think. It is ridiculously easy encrypt your boot drive and costs you nothing, and potentially saves you from months of headache.

There are several encryption apps at your disposal: the paid programs, such as PGP, Drivecrypt, and Phonecrypt, and the popular free versions, PGP and Truecrypt. There are a few differences between them but the one thing to take away from both free and paid versions is that they prohibit anyone from booting your computer, laptop, or phone without the password.

Truecrypt is free, and does this by creating a 256 AES encryption key. You install the application, select your drive you want to encrypt, and select your passphrase and create an encrypted key. Simple.

How does this benefit you? Well, the next time that thief who stole your laptop tries to boot up the hard drive, without the password he'll be out of luck. He is presented with this password field before windows even boots, and if it is not keyed in correctly, the drive halts. The password, if sufficiently long, is enough to withstand almost any brute-force attack, even by the NSA. Just make sure to use a passphrase that will be easy to remember, but long enough to thwart any attacker: 15-character passphrase with upper/lowercase letters with a number or two.

Just how strong is Truecrypt? It is considered impossible to crack, on the order of millions of years. It would take quantum computers eons to crack even a moderately length passphrase using brute-force methods. In all likelihood the absolute weakest link is *you*.

Keyloggers can obtain your password if you are unlucky enough to get one. However, these are a fairly rare occurrence if you keep your operating system, anti-virus and anti-malware programs up to date. The other weakest link is your passphrase. You would be surprised at just how many people use their own personal information in their passphrases. Doing this might make the password easier to remember, but also easier to crack.

A good passphrase is made up of lower and upper case characters in addition to spaces, which lend more entropy bits to the protection. At each instance a bit is added to a passphrase, the computational crunching requirement to crack such passphrase is doubled. If I were living in North Korea or China, for example, I would seriously consider a passphrase that was at least twenty characters long, with some keyboard symbols thrown in for good measure. Most people do not like to remember a twenty character passphrase however, so they use a less random one.

Drivecrypt is another encryption program, but it is not open-source and is not free. I have used this program for eight years and have to say if money is a concern, then go with Truecrypt as it has many of the same functions that Truecrypt does, and for zero cost. Drivecrypt has an option called "bootauth" which is short for boot authorization. The install process is similar to Truecrypt, though the bootup passphrase screen is a little different. You boot your hard drive, and then type in the passphrase to boot the OS. Truecrypt has this function as well.

As stated, it is not open-source. What that means is that it cannot be studied by the public sector (read: security users) to determine if any backdoors have been coded in. Like Truecrypt, it offers the option to create an encrypted operating system that holds a hidden operating system as well whose existence can be denied to those trying to harm or prosecute you. This is especially beneficial if you live in the UK, where failure to hand over a passphrase to an encrypted hard drive can get you two years in prison on a contempt of court charge. However you could give them the password to your decoy system. There is no way they could know if you were concealing a hidden operating system without a keylogger in place.

Truecrypt and Drivecrypt give no hints or leak any data regarding the existence of hidden files. The only way to mount said file is to know the password, and there are two you create with such an option: one for the decoy, and one for the hidden container/operating system.

Truecrypt and Drivecrypt also support the use of encrypted container files, which when clicked will mount the file the same way a mounting application like DaemonTools or Nero mounts an iso image. Prior to mounting, the application will ask you for the password. Mistype the password and the container does not mount at all. This can be very handy as there are a plethora of private items that you could conceal from government or any kind of prosecuting institution, such as medical records, tax records, school transcripts, business correspondence and the like.

Veracrypt may also be an option if you don't mind the Truecrypt interface. In fact, they look and act very similar.

VeraCrypt main features:

• Creates a **virtual encrypted disk** within a file and mounts it as a real disk.

• Encrypts an **entire partition or storage device** such as USB flash drive or hard drive.

• Encrypts a **partition or drive where Windows is installed** (pre-boot authentication).

• Encryption is **automatic**, **real-time**(on-the-fly) and **transparent**.

• Parallelization and pipelining allow data to be read and written as fast as if the drive was not encrypted.

• Encryption can be hardware-accelerated on modern processors.

• Provides **plausible deniability**, in case an adversary forces you to reveal the password: **Hidden volume** (steganography) and **hidden operating system**.

SOME TIPS FOR TRUECRYPT/VERACRYPT users:

1.) If you have one, disable the firewire port, as this can be used to reveal the encryption keys.

2.) Never leave any containers mounted on a laptop when crossing a border station, unless you want your private information in said container to be shared with the guards.

3.) Never leave your PC powered on and unattended for any lengthy amount of time (public wifi spots, cafes, libraries, college classrooms, etc). All security goes out the window when an attacker (or anyone else) has physical access to your machine. Neither Truecrypt nor Drivecrypt can protect your data in such a case, as the attacker can install a keylogger that can record your keystrokes.

Thumbnails

IF YOU POSSESS any incriminating snapshots (flings, Wikileak photos, informant docs) then at a later time delete the images in the folder, be aware that a shadow copy still exists. In windows XP (yes, legions of users are still clinging to this OS), thumbnails of jpegs are stored within each folder of the image's location. So if you have a folder called "government office snapshots", you will have thumbnails enabled in the folder settings tab for any pictures (jpegs, bitmaps, etc), and a hidden thumbs.db file will be present that shows a mini version of the picture in question. So even if you delete the jpegs, this hidden file will still reveal to anyone what the contents of the original folder were.

The only way to see or disable this hidden file is to go to Tools – Options – View and set the option to "show hidden files and folders".

Until this is done, every single folder with pictures in it will store a mini-snapshot of the pictures unless this is disabled. Windows 7 is a completely different file system to Windows XP. Instead of keeping the thumbnail cache within the folder where the pictures reside, it stores it in a central location

(%userprofile%\AppData\Local\Microsoft\Windows\Explorer)

I HAVE FOUND it much better to just leave the thumbnail option off in Windows 7, as the images load fairly quickly without the need for a cache to speed things up. There are other files, like text, audio and the like, that are also at risk of being discovered if you do not take precautions to securely delete the file. That does not mean deleted from the *recycle bin*, however. When you delete any items from the recycle bin, all that does is tell the operating system that the space previously occupied by that file can be written to again. It does not delete the file permanently until that space is overwritten to again by some other program.

Government agencies have programs that can *undelete* a file. The way around this is to use various programs to securely delete a file, such as Ccleaner. This app has an interesting wipe utility as well, in that it can wipe the free space of any previously deleted contents on the hard drive. You can even do this while the operating system is in use.

Needless to say, if you have a 2 terabyte hard drive and you're only using 20% of the drive, with 80% being "free space", then it will be a few hours for it to finish the wipe process, dependent on the speed of the hard drive and what other programs you have running. It does not touch any installed programs that exist already on the system unless you tell it to, and then only that free space that is allo-cated for use.

Swap File

LET'S TALK briefly about the "swap" file that most operating systems use. What this means is that sometimes during heavy PC usage, you will run low on system memory, and then the operating system will use your hard drive as a temporary ram storage device. This is what is called the "swap file", which increases the speed of computer operations. This swap file can be a veritable gold mine of data to someone with nefarious intentions.

Text files, video thumbnails, and word document fragments can exist herein, enough to print out a pretty good snapshot of your past. There have even been court cases where people were convicted in court using nothing but thumbnail fragments.

You can disable the swap file windows uses by going to control panel, System & Security, System, Advanced, Performance, Settings, Advanced, Virtual Memory and click Change. Choose "No Paging File". Reboot.

Note: Some resource intensive games use the swap file to speed up their games when there is not enough ram. If you run into any slowdowns with normal PC usage you can always switch this option back on, then reboot.

I2P

I2P, otherwise known as the "Invisible Internet Project" is another option that people can use to hide their online IP address. It shares a lot of the same characteristics of other networks in that it routes traffic through neighboring peers. The developers have stated that their main goal is not necessarily one of 100% anonymity (a goal some say is impossible), but rather to make the system too troubling and expensive to attack from the outside. It is an *anonymizing* network with several layers of encryption wrapped around all the data that travels through the system.

I2P VS Tor

YOU MIGHT THINK this sounds a lot like Freenet, but the similarity is actually more like Tor's network. I2P offers interactivity with websites, blogs, forums, chat, search engines and all without the need to install any of them locally. Such are the hallmarks of I2P. Websites that exist in the I2P network are called Eepsites, and are hosted anonymously with I2P being a strict requirement to access these websites. In that vein, it is similar to the .onion sites accessible only via Tor. Every PC that is connected to the I2P network shares in the forwarding of encrypted packets of data through proxies prior to the final destination. Each *subsequent* proxy prunes a layer of encryption at various intervals until encryption is removed. The bottom line is this: No one knows the origin of said packets, a trait also shared by Tor. While it is true that both Tor and I2P have different goals in mind, there exists many similarities:

- Both exist as anonymizing networks
- Both use layered encryption to funnel data
- Both have hidden services
- Tor has Exit Nodes and I2P has Outproxies

Benefits of Tor over I2P

- LARGER USER BASE THAN I2P; support from academic sources, constant improvements in stability and resistance to attacks
- Funding is sourced from many countries around the globe
- Large number of Exit Nodes
- Translated into many languages
- Optimized for Exit Traffic
- Memory more optimized than I2P
- Written in C

Benefits of I2P over Tor

- HIDDEN SERVICES much faster than the Tor network.
- Not as many DOS (denial of service) attacks as Tor.
- Compatible with peer-to-peer file sharing (Tor is not).
- Tor tunnels last a long time compared to I2P. This ensures less attacks as the number of samples a hacker may use are limited.
- Every peer routes data for others.

- Offers TCP/UDP.
- Written in Java.

AS YOU CAN SEE, both networks are safe enough for anonymity, as long as you aren't a world-hunted target. To this, a user's anonymity is typically broken due to their own sloppy behavior--their overconfidence being the weakest link in most cases (using the same login names on many websites, mixing these with Tor and non-Tor websites, and enabling JavaScript/Flash).

Since I2P is not built to act as a proxy to the WWW, you should use Tor if you want to surf anonymously. The outproxies on I2P, as you've probably guessed, are similar to the exit nodes on Tor, but they do not have the greatest support and tend to be unstable. Thus you should use Tor for anonymous web browsing and I2P for I2p eepsites. One option is to use Foxy Proxy to test it yourself. Be aware however that since there are fewer outproxies than Tor exit nodes, it may be easier for an adversary to identify your activities. It all depends on how much risk you want to assume and what the ramifications are if you are caught (and in which country).

You can also use I2P for BitTorrent and iMule as well as other P2P applications. Like Freenet, you will find that I2P will grow in speed the longer you use it without interruption. Torrents will be faster. Data will come down like lightning. Tor users will thank you for it. There are already too many torrent users on Tor that clog the network and make it difficult for people in dire straits who need anonymity for their political actions far more than the next Incubus CD.

While I2P is a technical powerhouse for anonymity, it can be a bit like a house of cards. Once the Ace is pulled from the bottom layer (by you), it can be rendered moot. I2P is just a tool, as is Tor and Freenet. It is not an invisibility cloak. Do something stupid, like move too much when a pack of Orcs are looking your way, you're bound to get an arrow in a place where you least expect it. Thus, act smart by being proactive in anonymity:

1.) TURN OFF JAVASCRIPT

Yes, it bears repeating, with arms waving in the air and shouting at the top of our lungs. Javascript is the bane of not only Tor, but other networks that rely on cloaking your IP address. Leaving this beastly plugin ON allows code to be run on your machine, code that will decloak you. Look at your browser settings and disable it. Also disable cookies. Super cookies are deployed in the wild to track down Tor users. Don't let it happen to you on I2P. Javascript can reveal a ton of metrics that fingerprint a user. Display resolution, page width, font and so on can be sent to an adversary by stealth. If you're in doubt, take a look at the web API at Mozilla:

HTTPS://DEVELOPER.MOZILLA.ORG/EN-US/DOCS/WEB/API

2.) SILENCE IS GOLDEN!

DON'T SAY A PEEP. Sure, you can talk. But refrain from discussing: the weather, your geography, your hobbies, your city politician that was just arrested for soliciting hookers. If someone says, "Hows the weather in your town?" You say: "Sunny." Every time. Alternatively, you may misinform. The CIA does it, why can't you? Their entire organization is built on secrecy and deception. Don't get too choked up about a few white lies. Spreading misinformation about trivial things like the weather and the local politics can really put a nail in an adversary's coffin. Ditto on employment. If you are asked about your work and you're a programmer, say you're a mail sorter down at the Post Office. They're not going to ask you about the latest Elvis stamp.

3.) ROTATE USERNAMES/NICS

The desire for convenience often gets people in trouble. They use the same usernames on multiple sites/forums. That's fine for the daytime, open web. Not so much for the darknet. It breaks anonymity. Take forums for example. When your username becomes infamous for a wealth of knowledge, change it. Create a new one. Don't tell anyone. Entropy rises when many users swap information like this on a frequent basis. Maintain separate personas: one for the darknet, one for regular internet. Memorization is better than writing it down.

4.) NEVER TURN **off your router**

I never turn mine off. Ever. If it is constantly going on and off while Freenet, Tor, I2P or IRC is running, after a while clues will surface as to who I really am, provided a sufficiently determined adversary has the resources to do it (NSA). The cost in power is negligible, so don't go cheap with anonymity. As the saying goes: out of speed, anonymity and reliability, you can only pick two, but make up for the lost component by acting *smart*.

5.) POWER IN NUMBERS: **Bandwidth**

Don't be stingy with your connection. The more you participate in the storm of users (Freenet, I2P), the more cloaked you will be. It is better to run 24/7 if you can. This makes it more difficult for an adversary to discern if you sent a file to someone else, or if you are merely the middle man to some file sent by a total unknown on the other side of the globe. Besides this, leaving the program running just makes it a lot faster network in general for other users. Think *Safety in Numbers*.

6.) OPTIONAL **(but smart)**

In the browser settings, set browser.safebrowsing.enabled and browser.safebrowsing.malware.enabled to false. Search goliaths like Google and Microsoft do not need to know the website URLs you visit.

Get into the habit of flushing the cache--cookies, etc. You can set this to do it automatically upon exit of the browser.

Refrain from using Foxy Proxy to selective proxy .i2p links. You don't want to be sent to the clearnet. If an I2P website is a honeypot, your Firefox browser can send a unique identifier in the referrer, in which case... anonymity broken.

At this point you're probably thinking this is way more headaches than it is worth. And you'd be right...in the beginning. But anything worth doing is usually hard at the outset. I as well as my colleagues do all of these things only because we have done them for years.

We do them every day.

Are we thinking about them?

No, not in the least on account of smart habits done daily. Do you think intently about starting your car? Pulling out of the driveway? No. But it's a good bet you were petrified to do it when you were sixteen. And pulling out of your driveway is a very complex action, as are the aforementioned suggestions. Just one of your brain cells is more complex than a 747. Don't waste any of them.

Torrents and Eepsites

FIRST THINGS FIRST. Install not only the NoScript plugin, but also the Cookie Whitelist (Buttons). Ideally you want to block everything when surfing Eepsites. There are a multitude of add-ons on the

Firefox site but you do not need all of them. You only need the ones that preserve your anonymity.

INSTALL QUICKPROXY, also at the Firefox site. Restart. Then open the proxy settings using the edit tab and then browse to "Preferences" and "Advanced". Then "Settings". Change your proxy settings to:

127.0.0.1 for HTTP Proxy, Port 4444 and 127.0.0.1 and port 4445 for SSL Proxy. Ensure Socks v4 is checked.

CLICK "OKAY" and exit out. If you've configured it correctly you should be able to click the QuickProxy icon (lower corner of browser) when you browse Eepsites. You can also paste in .i2p websites and hit "Go" the old fashioned way.

Torrents

AN OPTION for torrents is to use I2PSnark. If you're a beginner, ensure the service is running by opening a terminal and inputing:

$ I2PROUTER STATUS

IF IT IS NOT RUNNING, start it with:

$ I2PROUTER STATUS

THEN BROWSE via Firefox to

HTTP://LOCALHOST:7657/I2PSNARK/

AT THE MAIN I2PSNARK PAGE, you can see it running. Now you can create a torrent. Move a torrent and the data into

~/.I2P/I2PSNARK

THE OTHER OPTION is to paste the data you want to seed to the same directory, and in my case, this is usually PDFs and technical manuals. At the Tracker option, you can choose whatever method you wish or create an entirely new torrent. I2PSnark will create the new torrent and set it in a queue. All that remains to be done is to click Start in the top corner and away you go.

Get your torrents from Postman's tracker:

HTTP://TRACKER2.POSTMAN.I2P/

TORRENTS MIGHT BE slow at first, but do not get discouraged. You will have far faster downloads on I2P than you ever will Tor. One can never have enough good karma in this world.

FACEBOOK AND OTHER MISFITS

Facebook is a bit of a mixed bag where ethics is concerned. On the one hand, it is immensely popular and profit-inducing for a reason: people love to chat with relatives, old neighborhood friends, girl-friends, mistresses and political liaisons, all in real-time. People love connections. The feeling of unity and solidarity. The benefits are fairly immediate if you're the type of individual who likes instant gratification. There is nothing quite like the feeling of seeing old friends on your friend's list who you have not seen in twenty-five years, now instantly accessible for a chat session at just about any time of day.

It used to be that Facebook didn't rely as much on the IP address as a P2P network did. Times have changed. Nowadays, all of your personal information is theirs for the taking, and in some cases offered up on a digital platter by endusers. Your real name, phone number, who your past and present friends are, and even your pets are all valuable data as it can be targeted with advertising tailored to every atom of your personality. What could go wrong, you ask?

One problem facing Facebook users is that it is all too easy for Facebook to give this treasure trove of data up to the highest bidder.

Worse, Facebook acts not as a protector of the 4th amendment, but as an destroyer of it. Many government agencies and local law enforcement have relied on Facebook profiles to establish alibis, reveal private emails, and prove or disprove acts that may be criminal or not. Read the Facebook privacy policy for yourself:

"WE MAY ALSO SHARE information when we have a good faith belief it is necessary to prevent fraud or other illegal activity, to prevent imminent bodily harm, or to protect ourselves and you from people violating our Statement of Rights and Responsibilities. This may include sharing information with other companies, lawyers, courts or other government entities."

THEY'RE MANDATED by the government to abide by subpoenas for user information data except any private messages that are unopened and are less than 181 days of age (these require a warrant). The problem is that the Supreme Court never recognized a 4th amendment right to privacy. That is, data being shared with third parties, so the government pretty much has a blank check to engage in "shooting-fish-in-a-barrel" type expeditions for subscriber information that may or may not have anything to do with any criminal acts.

State and corporation are thus conjoined at the hip in a quasi-fascism that is difficult to defeat and predict, nevermind the fact that the government often, when it has nothing else to do, creates laws that are meant to be broken--over and over (speed limits, anyone?).

Thus, outside of discussions on anonymity, there is a not much to do when the enemy's archers are standing upon the castle towers with flaming arrows aimed at the exposed king. But we'll try nevertheless.

Be mindful of what you type on Facebook. Actually, be paranoid, unless you are one of the king's fools. This should go without saying, but the neverending stream of fools on Facebook often don't even recognize your need for privacy or anonymity to say nothing of their own. They get so accustomed to the personalized interface that you start to think they've got in it for you with their shouting your real name across the internet.

You are not anonymous here, or on any other social media site-- Twitter, Pinterest, Google Plus, etc.

In fact, a new Facebook account has even less privacy than one on a P2P network like Emule. Where emule is concerned, you only had to worry about the ip address. With Facebook, your private life belongs to them unless you take drastic action to prevent it. Yes, you may have heard more than a few complaints from a few peasants about the lack of privacy on Social Media. It hasn't failed to reached the ears of the ivory tower executives at Facebook, Inc. But what do they really think of anonymity?

THE ANOMALY: **Anonymous Facebook Login**

IN APRIL OF 2014, CEO Mark Zuckerberg announced that Facebook planned to implement "Anonymous Login" for all users. It was a misnomer in the same way that "cat owner" is a misnomer. It offers more privacy, certainly, but not anonymity. It doesn't come close to anonymity since you cannot login to Facebook *anonymously*. What it means is that, using your Facebook login, you can sign in to other websites, say at Ars Technica or Wired, and make comments without having to grant access to the treasure of data Facebook holds on you: your list of contacts, relatives, friends, favorite cereals and the fact you hate cats with a brimstone passion.

Presently they are testing this so called "anonymity" service with a smattering of social sites and forums so as to better "benefit the end-user", as Zuckerberg claims--grant more control to its userbase on some of the data that gets transferred. Notice the word "some"... of the data. Not all.

And herein is the fallacy: most people, especially those on social media, do not know the difference between anonymity and privacy. Thus the masses will gobble it up. Certainly signing up for a new service can be cumbersome--email, check link, clink on link, fill out forms, click another link in email, fill out more forms. It's a breath of fresh air to know simpler times are in the pipeline, but let's call it what is: efficiency, not anonymity.

Most people will think Facebook will stand true to their anonymity statement, but the truth of it is that they lied to their user-base right out of the gate, trading the mundane term *privacy* for the much loftier goal of *anonymity*. Facebook knows all about these third party sites you visit, and is willing to offer the data up to the highest bidder.

Your behavior, your identity, your favorites, all are a win-win for Facebook, and a lose-lose for the third party sites and *you*. If a nosy judge wants to uncloak you on a third party site over some "slander-ous" comment you made, they need not go to the third party site. They will go to Facebook. They know the name you signed in with, the time you made the comment, the IP address you used to bounce to the discussion. Checkmate.

In an interview with Wired's Steve Levy, Zuckerberg had this to say about their new vision:

"WHEN WE WERE A SMALLER COMPANY, Facebook login was widely adopted, and the growth rate for it has been quite quick. But in order to get to the next level and become more ubiquitous, it needs to be trusted even more. We're a bigger company now and people have more questions. We need to give people more control over their information so that everyone feels comfortable using these products."

SOUNDS SUSPICIOUS, does it not? Well, that's not to say it's good for the goose either. In this case, the third party. Website developers who decide to use Facebook's API to expand their readership will have that decision come back to haunt them since Facebook "controls" the client that uses the API login. They can shut off the API for the developers just as Nevada can shut off water piping out to California. To counter this, they will be ever more vigilant in mining user data and be hesitant, if not fully opposed, to using this new "anonymous" setting as it grants Facebook absolute rule over its userbase. That is, if they were *smart*. Many are not.

HOW TO BE **Anonymous on Facebook**

FACEBOOK IS ALLERGIC TO ANONYMITY. You've probably heard that they frown on anonymous accounts. It is not entirely difficult to understand why. They can't target you with advertisements if they don't know who you are, and that's their bread and butter. From your behavior come the metrics, the things you buy, the places you enjoy visiting, your family links. From their own lips:

"WE REQUIRE everyone to provide their real names, so you always know who you're connecting with."

THIS IS a roadblock that fortunately can be overcome, since genuine names are not yet tied to any form of government ID schemes like driver's licenses or social security numbers (though they will be someday). And even then, the rules of supply and demand would dictate even this would not dissuade the need for full anonymity.

When you are neck-deep in the account creation process at Facebook, you need to enter as much false data as you can. The email address in particular needs to be created in complete anonymity. The big mistake most people make is assuming that clocking the IP address is a sufficient means to the end. However there are many tracking mechanisms--complex algorithms designed to match behavior patterns and preferential choices--that all the big social media giants employ. Just one slip up, a broken link in the chain such as connecting to a website that knows your real identity (BBC, for instance) can destroy your every effort. Before you know it, all the others have been alerted by bots, warning pings and moderators that you've talked to in that session. Endgame.

Ask yourself this: Would your closest friends refer to you by name if you attended a popular masquerade in New Orleans during Mardi Gras? You bet they would, masked or not, even if you had pleaded with them to protect your identity. Some of them might whisper your name, not really even thinking about their prior oath of secrecy.

Then before you know it, another who happens to have the ears of a fox overhears your name being called. In much the same way, Facebook identifies you by your acquaintances just as others might do at the masquerade. Who is he talking to? A woman? Young or old? Tall or short? Do they talk with their hands? Ah, that's Maria from Rome. It's really not too difficult, and neither is it for Facebook. Friends and family lists are hardline identifiers in Facebook and Google's algorithms. The facial recognition Facebook employs can only get more advanced as it scours the web for matches elsewhere: Flickr. Google. Amazon. Twitter. Mugshot sites. Surveillance videos. Then there are photos of you to worry about: photos your friends have that are out of your control.

Facebook installs super cookies on your machine (or one of their many 3rd party enforcers) that tracks you in a number of ways: by Sid number, MAC address, etc. It continues to track you even after you've logged out of all your social media sites. There can be no such event as 100% anonymity just as there can be no such thing as a perfect human. We are the weak links.

But fear not, young Jedi. All is not yet lost.

While true anonymity is difficult, it is not impossible. We can approach 98% anonymity with some smart decisions. First things first. Invest in a VPN account. The more walls we have between us and the target, the stronger the cloak. Visibility is cloudy in a VPN as they shield many of your moves. Location awareness is difficult to detect using a VPN, but avoid free public proxies as Facebook and every other site has been spammed to death with them and have shielded themselves from those range of IP addresses. Thus, a proper (well-respected) VPN is the way to go. You will want speed to blend in with other non-anonymous users. Every metric counts.

You will need to disable most cookies from third-parties but allow Facebook for each session. Using Firefox portable, you can set the browser to auto-clear them upon exiting each session.

Set up your false data. Everything must be different from anything you've set at any other forum. Ars Technica, Wired, WSJ-- they're all in bed with Facebook to one degree or another. Ensure complete uniqueness, and under no circumstances give them your mobile phone number, as this will nuke your anonymity before it gets off the ground. That number, along with the IP, is used primarily for targeted advertising as well as by law enforcement. You may have noticed that Yahoo now requires it for new accounts. The reason is that it makes things easier to identify you.

Avoid a large group of friends and NO RELATIVES. This can't be stressed enough. Relatives, especially the elderly, love to gossip and spill details about the retched veal you cooked last night, or the cat you sprayed with the garden hose last week. What you don't hear in other's chat boxes at Facebook can harm you. Politely tell (never ask) others not to tag you or refer to any events that may compromise you: pictures, videos, music that your "real self" enjoys. Three bread-crumbs is enough to raise the eyebrow of the algorithm. Insist on them calling you by a nickname. If they refuse, remove them.

Never use the same browser for your VPN that you use for non-VPN sessions. Install Firefox portable in its own directory with its own shortcut and configured to the VPN BEFORE creating the

Facebook account. Never mix them up. You don't want cross-cookie contamination.

Be cautious on other social sites as well: Google, Twitter, Pinterest, MySpace. Facebook will not invest in the resources to find you unless you hand them crumbs of data yourself, which can easily be done on other sites you are careless with. So avoid being too specific about things related to your hardwired beliefs on those other sites, too: Religion. Politics. Ethics. Switch them up. Be a Buddhist for a session or two. Or a non-practicing non-denominationalist. Just be mindful of stirring up a hornet's nest. A friend in Thailand (an American) who was well known in Freenet insulted the Thai king on Facebook, prompting them to take a magnifying glass to his account. The end result? Facebook changed his name without his authorization--to reflect his *real identity*. Embarrassing. He'd posted a link to his page on Freenet as well and as you can imagine, his entire identity was uncovered by this loud behavior.

It is not possible to convert your existing Facebook profile into an anonymous one no matter how many tweaks you make. Changing the name will do nothing. The algorithm (think of the sentinels from The Matrix) will still have records of your online behavior as well as your IP address. Privacy, however, *is* obtainable, in case you wish to shield your identity from nosy coworkers or other misfits. In this case you need to change your username, that part of the profile others see then tweak the privacy settings accordingly with how invisible you wish to be. It is a bit of a double-edged sword since this will make it harder for others to see you--those you may *wish* to see you. You'll have to seek them out yourself and add them. And this, too, can reveal your true identity. Nothing typed into Facebook is ever truly invisible from the bots at their disposal.

TAILS

Edward Snowden. The name rings a bell for most people around the globe. In tech circles he is a visionary. As for the non-techies, a few labels come to mind: Whistleblower. Hero. Traitor. Regardless of what you pin him with, one thing is certain: He hates censorship and loves anonymity, the kind of anonymity that calls for untrackable execution. Before discussing anything, he insisted liaisons use not only PGP (pretty good privacy) but the end-all-be-all of anonymity tools:

Tails

It is a simple tool that frustrates even those in the upper echelon of the NSA. And for good reason, since even they do not know the wizard who designed it.

Where Tor is the worm of the anonymous fisherman, Tails is the fishing box. The fish at the other end have no idea who is inside the boat, watching, listening. It's a hacker's tool but also a patriot weapon. Using it is a breeze: install it on a USB stick, CD, whatever, boot from said stick and find yourself cloaked and shielded from the NSA, provided that you don't out yourself. And if you're using Tails, you're smarter than that anyway.

Built upon the shell of Linux, it acts as an operating system and comes with an assortment of nukes to launch under Big Brother's nose: Tor browser, chat client, email, office suite and image/sound editor, among others.

Snowden preferred Tails on account of its no-write rule: no direct data writing. A breach from a remote adversary? Not going to happen. Forensics investigation? Nope. No trace is going to be left on the DVD/USB. Obviously this is a no brainer to use if you're an NSA employee looking to spill the beans on unconstitutional spying, as well as a must-have for political dissidents and journalists. It is armored with plausible deniability, the same as Truecrypt.

Tor runs like warm butter when you boot with Tails. There's not much of a learning curve, and no excessive tweaking required. You can use it in the same PC you use at work. Boot from USB or DVD. Do your thing then reboot back into your normal PC with no record or footprint of your Tailing. For all intents, you're a ghost on the internet. And speaking of ghosts, the creators of Tails are anonymous themselves. No one knows their identities. But what we do know is that they will not bow to governments trying to muscle a backdoor into the code.

Linus Torvalds, creator of Linux, said in 2013, "The NSA has been pressuring free software projects and developers in various ways," implying that they had made the effort, and all with taxpayer funds. A bit like the cat saying to the mouse, "Transparency is good for you. Sleep out in the open and not the damp and dark, flea-infested mousehole." They don't like secrets.

You might be asking, how do we *know* that Tails does not already *have* a backdoor? How do we know that the NSA has not already greased their hands? The evidence is twofold: the code is open-source (anyone can audit it), and the mere fact that the NSA made an effort to sideline end-users says they fear such a powerful package. They cannot peer inside to see what the mice are doing. Snowden claimed that the NSA, while he was with them, was a major thorn in the side of that organization.

At the time of Tails conception five years ago, the interest had already started to build up in the Tor community for a more cohesive toolbox. "At that time some of us were already Tor enthusiasts and had been involved in free software communities for years," they said. "But we felt that something was missing to the panorama: a toolbox that would bring all the essential privacy enhancing technologies together and made them ready to use and accessible to a larger public."

PGP is also included in package. You owe it to yourself and peace of mind to learn it. Spend a Sunday with it and you'll be a competent user. Spend a week and you'll be an enthusiast.

As well, KeePassX can be useful if you want to store different info (usernames, pass phrases, sites, comments) into one database. These two are like a good set of gauntlets no aspiring black knight would do without. And don't think the blacksmiths have just smelted down some cheap metal, either. The designers have gone to a lot of trouble to modify the privacy and security settings. The more they do, the less you have to.

This is not to say you should use Tails every day. Only use it in those times you feel anonymity is warranted. As mentioned before, if you start mixing up services, operating systems and mac addresses, you may blow your cover. Though Tails is packaged with programs that one wouldn't normally associate with anonymity (GIMP, Open-Office, Audacity, etc) you don't want to leak info where an adversary might build a profile on you. You'd be shocked at how many applications these days "dial home" without your knowledge (hint: almost all of them).

But the true Achilles heel is the *metadata*. Tails is really lousy at hiding it. It doesn't try to. It doesn't clear any of it nor does it encrypt the headers of your encrypted emails. Are you an ebook author? Be careful about PDFs and .mobi files, as depending on which software you use, it can store the author's name and creation date of your work. But this is not really the fault of Tails. Rather, it is the wishes of the development team to stay compatible with the SMTP protocol.

The other problem with metadata is pictures: JPEGs, TIFF, BITMAPS and so on, which again, depending on the software, can store EXIF data--data that stores the date the picture was taken as well as the GPS coordinates of the image. Newer cameras and mobile phones like Samsung Galaxy are notorious for this, and even keep a thumbnail of the EXIF data intact for nose parkers with nothing to do all day but to sniff through other people's property. A fake GPS spoofer may be useful but even that won't eliminate the exif data. You'll need a separate app for this. You might even go so far as to only use formats that don't store any metadata at all. Plain-text is one option, though even that can be watermarked.

You might think, "Can I hide Tails activity?" The short answer is: maybe. It depends on the resources of the adversary. And just who is the adversary? The government? The private detective? The employer? The fingerprint Tails leaves is far less visible than what Tor leaves. And yes, it is possible for an administrator to see you are using Tor, as well as your ISP. They cannot tell what you're doing on Tor, mind you, but there are Tor Browser Bundle users, and Tails users. It all comes down to the sites you visit.

We've seen how they can build a profile on you from your resolution, window metrics, addons and extensions and time zones and fonts, but to alleviate this the Tails developers have tried to make everyone look the same, as if they were all wearing white Stormtrooper armor. Some fall through the cracks, making themselves easier for a correlation attack by installing too many addons and thus marking themselves in the herd: A purple-colored stormtrooper, if you will. Such and such user has a nice font enhancer while no other user does. This alone does not break anonymity, but with a hundred other factors and sufficient resources, it might be the one detail that breaks the house of cards. Death by a thousand stings.

You might find Tor bridges (alternative entry points on Tor) to be a good investment in reading, as they can better hide you from your ISP. In fact, using a bridge makes it considerably harder for your ISP to even know you are using Tor. If you decide this route (and you should if merely using Tor can get you arrested-- a case in which you should NOT use the default Tor configuration), the bridge address must be known.

Be mindful of the fact that a few bridges can be obtained on the Tor website. If you know about it, others do too--even adversaries like the NSA, but it is still stronger for anonymity purposes than the default Tor config. Like Freenet, it would be optimal if you personally know someone in a country outside the USA who runs a private obfuscated bridge that has the option *PublishServerDescriptor* o. As always, luck favors the prepared.

HOW TO DEFEAT THE NSA

It needs to be said: The time is nigh for the NSA to dissolve. If not dissolved, then at least broken up as Nazi Germany was after WWII. Yeah I hear your eyes rolling. Comparing the Nazis again? Please.

But mission creep, the expansion of a project beyond its original goals (often after initial successes) has reared its ugly head once again as the NSA, once known as "No Such Agency", has far surpassed its original purpose: to secure American communications while gathering intel on our enemies. Unfortunately, it seems *we* have become the enemy. We, the path of least resistance, so to speak.

Intelligence gathering is now such a high priority to the NSA that it has gone global at the expense of sovereign security. The Tailored Access Operations (TAO) directive makes this obvious. Install spyware/backdoors on the enemy's computers... well and good until Snowden revealed that they do the same to their own countrymen. It's called *bulk surveillance*. The more data they have, the louder they are on claiming victory over the usual boogeymen: Terrorists. Drug lords. (how long was it to catch Bin Laden?). Emails, calls, even video is collected without your consent. You could say it is a system ripe for abuse, if it were not already rotting from the inside out due to the

Patriot Act (section 215). The very notion that the NSA can shield itself from Congress and the taxpayers who foot the bill should appall most Americans.

So, what to do when the mother eagle turns on her chicks? Answer: Build your own nest. First things first, however. Understand that if you are a high value target like Bin Laden or a Mafia don, the NSA will hack your internet-connected computer or phone regardless. There's no getting around it. If you're thinking, "Well, I paid a hundred clams for Drivecrypt and Phonecrypt and so it is safe from those hucksters," there is some bad news for you to swallow, cowboy. It is far from safe.

Drivecrypt is commercial software and closed-source, and considering the free offerings out there (Truecrypt--open-source and *audited*), the best case would be that you're only paying for the name. Worst case? The NSA has a backdoor within the code, or at least knows of an exploit no one else knows about. You can thank the NSA's BULLRUN program, which attempts to "insert vulnerabilities into commercial encryption systems, IT systems, networks and endpoint communication devices."

In an ideal, pro-Constitution country, the security of the citizenry against foreign threats would be priority one. Instead, we are faced with a well-funded behemoth that considers the monitoring and data farming of *citizens* priority one. Again, think "least resistance". Hacked accounts from Blizzard to Kickstarter to Yahoo occur every month and the NSA seems helpless to stop it. Only the truth is a little different than they led us to believe.

They do have the means to stop it, as it turns out. But it would require a significant rerouting of resources so that citizens are protected and not monitored and assumed guilty of some obscure crime. Worse, the positions of authority and influence are unbalanced and skewed. Cyber Command should not be integrated with NSA priorities at all. Their priorities should be focused abroad, *like all other military operations*, and not focused on citizens like some Eye of Sauron that creates crime out of thin air.

Luckily, a few have leaked enough data from the NSA's coffers to mount a counteroffensive. One man cannot undo the damage they've done, but a nation can: the millions can overpower their overreach and send them back to their proper place.

How?

Knowledge is power. This hardly changes over time and for the NSA, the knowledge resides in the network itself. That's where the NSA loves to probe and plant their bugs. To this, they farm all the data. Everything. Then hire analysts to sort it all. They monitor phone calls, satellite messages and even listen to the oceanic cables running to and fro to our allies. They tap the waterfall at the source, high above, or beneath our feet if need be. Good intel, ripe for the sifting.

But what is good intel to them? Well, it's whatever sets off the most flags: the people involved, their countries, the language they use, their religion. It all gets prioritized based on profiles their algo agents categorize. The more red flags, the higher up the totem pole it goes... into a wellspring of *metadata*. It is easier to cherry pick targets by examining metadata than to study complete emails and conversations. It saves time. It saves money. Metadata to the NSA is like cocaine to a drug dealer. It's valuable stuff.

The Systems Intelligence Directorate does the data sifting and sorting in this case, and is given billions by Congress to optimize its operations every year. They are always updating and honing their capabilities. Testing what works and what doesn't. A security group exists for each directive handed down by the brass. They do nothing but look for ways to streamline each infiltration tactic. Make it all blood simple with the push of a button, a button that has global outreach.

NSA agents can infiltrate at will, but they especially love non-updated hardware like routers. When was the last time you updated your router encryption key? Right. The NSA knows this as well. They have a backdoor for many of them and entire teams devoted 24/7 to finding exploits for every brand of router and password encryption scheme. This is all accomplished by the TAO (Tailored Access Operations). Once inside your PC, they can easily install a custom-made keylogger that records your keystrokes and will send them quietly under the radar. Your anti-virus will not detect it. Once this is done, it doesn't matter how complex your password is. Thus, it is easy to see how valuable prevention is.

But how does one prevent such an intrusion from a well-funded entity? The answer is **encryption**. Encrypt your email. Your data. Your boot pass phrase. Most people will not bother with email. Some might bother with data. And fewer still will bother with encrypting the entire OS as it can take hours for a 2 TB hard drive.

A few strict security suggestions:

I) The NSA does not like Tor. It's expensive to track users. When a lot of money is asked of Congress, they start asking questions and demanding results. They don't want *anyone* asking questions. So use Tor. However, do not say anything in an email that you would not recover from if it was broadcasted on network TV. And do not access your normal email account or bank account using Tor. Can you see why?

II.) Invest in an offline netbook or laptop for mission critical data. Make encrypted backups: Blu-Ray, USB, SD. Never allow the data onto your internet PC unless in encrypted form: Truecrypt containers/PGP encrypted, etc. Only decrypt messages offline and away from the internet. Learn about SSL/IPsec. Many Usenet providers offer SSL for free but leave it off by default. Turn it on.

III.) Whenever possible, avoid commercial encryption packages. The proprietary software is almost never audited, unlike Truecrypt. What does that tell you when they are afraid of people looking at their code? They're hiding something from you. When an encryption program is open-source, it is more secure, not less, because others can verify its security and detect any back doors. Word spreads like wildfire when a backdoor is discovered, but not if the door is nailed shut from the other side.

IV.) Your screen lock does not have to be perfect. It won't keep out any government agents but it may keep out nosy wives and friends. If however the OS is not encrypted and your laptop is stolen, all your data is theirs for the taking. Use an open-source app like Password Safe to secure them all from prying eyes.

You're probably thinking, why do you need all of these tools for privacy? Shouldn't Truecrypt or SSL for your Usenet be enough? The short answer is: it depends. It depends on your own level of risk. What you can live with if all is lost. And your loss is the NSA's gain, through threats of lawsuits and coercions and unconstitutional spying. They've almost succeeded in turning the web into a vast Orwellian looking glass-- with themselves as the only keymasters. They can only succeed if good men do nothing.

Trust encryption like you trust ammunition. And like ammunition, it can be learned in a weekend. Mastery however takes some time and effort, but know that by itself, it will do nothing but allow tyranny to flourish unless used for its original purpose.

Endgame

Hopefully if you have read this far, then you are now aware of some of the dangers that await us in the future. Clearly, having an exposed IP address is only a drop in the ocean next to the coming power grab. Unfortunately, there are always going to be up and coming social networks and applications that try to go above and beyond the use of the IP address to monitor you. We have seen it happen with many personal applications over the years: Internet Explorer, Napster, Limewire, Myspace, Facebook and the like.

These make their profits by subverting your personal choices and then targeting you based on those choices, and when you get right down to it, the longer you put off protecting your individuality, the less choice you will have in the long run. However, you now have at least an effective arsenal of tools in which to minimize this subversion. If enough people take notice, it may stem or even reverse the tide of fascism coming over the hills.

More and more we are seeing a gradual erosion of privacy. Some employers reject applicants to entry level positions based on credit score. Some employers demand Facebook usernames and passwords before hire. Some fire employees for words on a Facebook post. In the end it is all about control and eroding individual choice. For there is no one in the universe more unique than you. You are worth more than all the stars combined, and they know it. And want to control it. And there is no such thing as controlling just a little bit of a star.

Stay safe, always.

TOR & THE DARK ART OF ANONYMITY

TABLE OF CONTENT

PREFACE

You want what you want.

Invisibility. Anonymity. Ghost protocol.

You've taken the red pill and have seen the truth, and you don't like it. I don't blame you. I didn't like it either. But what I thought I knew about Tor and other incognito tools was only a drop in the ocean next to what's really out there. Stuff you don't find on many tech forums. They're whispered in private, of course, and it's all been rather invisible to you unless you hang out in hacker forums or Usenet. That is, until now.

Which brings us to you and I, or rather what I can do for you. It's amazing what a guy can learn in a decade when he rolls his sleeves up and gets his hands dirty. Private hacker forums. Usenet. Freenet. I scoured them all for years and what I've learned isn't anywhere else on Amazon.

Equally amazing is what you can learn for a few dollars in a weekend's worth of reading. That's me, and soon to be *you*. Where you will be by Monday is where I am now, only without the years of mistakes. Mistakes I made using Freenet, Tails, PGP. You name it, I did it. And boy did I make big ones: mistakes you'll avoid because after you read this guide, you'll know more than 85% of the Tor users out there, and know more about anonymity than most Federal agents. Yes, even the so-called super hackers at the NSA.

If you don't come away satisfied, return it for a full refund.

But I know you won't. Because once you've taken the red pill, there ain't no going back. You can't unlearn what you've learned, unsee what you've seen, and you'll want more. Much, much more.

First off, we're not sticking with the basics here. If all you want is Tor for Dummies, look elsewhere. Where we're going is dangerous territory. It's shark territory when you get right down to it. But not to worry. We've got shark repellant and everything you need to surf safe. You'll reap benefits you've only dreamed of and by the time we're done, you'll have gained NSA-level anonymity skills with a counter-surveillance mindset that rivals anything Anonymous or those goons at the NSA can counter with.

Speaking of which, they won't have a clue as to how to find you.

Secondly, for a few dollars you will know every exploit those superhackers like to wield against Tor users and more: How to avoid NSA tracking. Bitcoin anonymity (*real* anonymity), opsec advice and Darknet markets and Darkcoins and, well, it's a long list frankly but by the time you're done you'll be a Darknet *artist* when it comes to marketplaces and buying things incognito.

Third, we'll go over many techniques used by the CIA and FBI to entrap users. False confessions. Clickbait. Tor honeypots. It's all the same. You'll learn the same techniques used to catch terrorists, hackers and the group Anonymous and couriers for Reloaded. Baits and Lures and how to spot an LEA agent from a mile away. I break it all down into simple steps that you can understand. A few dollars for this info will save you a lifetime of grief. No, you won't find it on Reddit or Ars Technica or Wired. If you're mulling this over, don't. You need this now, not when you're framed for something you didn't do.

Fourth... reading the dangerous material herein requires you take action.

The Feds take action. Identity thieves take action. Hackers take action. Will you? Make no mistake - This is not a mere guide. It is a *mindset*. It's professional level stuff meant to keep you and your family safe for a decade out, going far beyond apps and proxies. And it's all yours if you do two simple things: You read, then act. Simple. Because you know what they say: Knowledge is power.

No, strike that. Knowledge is *potential* power. *Your* power. But only if you act.

Fifth... I update this book every month. New browser exploit in the wild? I update it here. New technique for uncloaking Tor users? You'll read it here first. We all know how Truecrypt is Not Safe Anymore, but that's only the beginning.

Besides, freedom isn't free.

Lastly... The scene from Jurassic Park with Dennis Nedry, I believe, is a nice frightful analogy to what happens if you don't take your security seriously. We see poor Dennis try to get his jeep out of the muck in the middle of a tropical storm. Lightning unzips the sky and the rain pours. The thunder rolls. A dilophosaur bounds upon him, beautiful, yet painted across his ugly mug is a deadly curiosity as it sniffs the air and cocks it's head at Nedry - moments before spraying his chubby eyes with poison. Blinded, he staggers back to the safety of the jeep, wailing and gnashing teeth, only to discover a visual horror to his right: he's left the passenger-side door ajar - wide enough to let Mr. Curious in for a juicy evening meal - which it savors with a row of sharp teeth.

The point is this: Don't be Dennis Nedry. There are far bigger creatures who'd like nothing better than to split your life (and family) wide open if for no other reason than they can. Such is the nature of the elite.

Unless, of course, you tame them...

Not bloody likely.

ONE

IS TOR SAFE?

That seems to be the question alright. And to that, well, it really depends on whom you ask because there are always wolves in sheep's clothing out there who stand to gain from a man's ignorance. Many say no. A few will say yes, that it's 'safe enough'. The media, for all their expertise in things political and social, come up woefully lacking when something as complex as Tor is discussed and get a lot of things wrong.

Case in point. Gizmodo reported that in December, 2014, a group of hackers managed to compromise enough Tor relays to de-cloak Tor users. If you're just hearing this for the first time, part of what makes Tor anonymous is that it relays your data from one node to another. It was believed that if they compromised enough of them, then they could track individual users on the Tor network and reveal their real life identities. Kind of like how the agents in The Matrix find those who've been unplugged.

Anyway as luck would have it, it turned out to be kiddie script-hackers with too much time on their hands who simply wanted a new target to hack. Who knows why. Could be that they'd toyed with the

Playstation Network and Xbox users long enough and simply wanted a curious peak here and there. These were not superhackers.

But as is usually the case with the media, this attack attracted the attention of a few bloggers and tech journalists unsympathetic to Tor and frankly, ignorant of what really constitutes a threat. The Tor devs commented on it, too:

"This looks like a regular attempt at a Sybil attack: the attackers have signed up many new relays in hopes of becoming a large fraction of the network. But even though they are running thousands of new relays, their relays currently make up less than 1% of the Tor network by capacity. We are working now to remove these relays from the network before they become a threat, and we don't expect any anonymity or performance effects based on what we've seen so far."

What those conspiracy bloggers failed to report was that any decentralized network like Tor is a prime target for attacks such as the above. But to truly stand a chance at punching a hole through this matrix, hackers would need Tor to implicitly trust every new node that comes online. That doesn't happen.

It also takes time for fresh relays to gather traffic - some as long as sixty days or more and the *likelihood* of being reported is rather high since the IP addresses are out in the open - which only speeds up malicious reporting. The *real* danger, and has been since inception, is scaring Tor users to less secure methods of communication. That's what the NSA wants. The CIA already does this in foreign countries. Now the NSA is following their lead.

TWO

RISKS OF USING TOR

The REAL Risk of Using Tor

I LIST them here before we dive deep into enemy territory so you'll know what to avoid before installation, and maybe get an "a-ha!" moment in subsequent chapters. As you read, remember that having Javascript on is really only a drop in the ocean next to what is possible for an enemy to kill your anonymity.

Javascript

It's widely known that leaving Javascript on is bad for a Tor user. Ninety-five percent of us know this, but the mistakes of the 5% get blown out of proportion and thrown into the face of the rest of us. Worse, many websites now run so many scripts that it seems as though they hate Tor users.

One site required over a dozen. Without it, the page was/is/will be pretty much gimped. Sometimes not even *readable*. You can imagine what might happen if you were using Tor and decided to visit that site if it was set up to lure users into a honeypot.

I remember one researcher claimed that "81% of Tor users can be de-anonymised."

Bull.

That 81% figure came about because the targeted users knew little about the NoScript browser add-on, and likely mixed Tor usage with their daily open net usage, providing ample data for a correlation attack. But that was just the icing on the cake. They left personal details *everywhere* - using the same usernames and passes they do elsewhere on the open net. Bragging about their favorite Netflix movies. Talking about local events (Jazzfest in New Orleans!). The weather (Hurricane in the French Quarter!). You get the idea.

Volunteering as an Exit Node

ANOTHER DOOZY, though not quite the granddaddy of all risks, but still risky. On the plus side, you as a valiant believer in anonymity graciously provide bandwidth and an "exit pipe" to the rest of the Tor users (hopefully none of whom you know) so that they may pass their encrypted traffic through your node. Generous? Certainly. Wise? If you live in the States... hale no as my Uncle Frick in Texas used to say.

It isn't that it is illegal *per se* to do so. On the contrary, but what passes through your node can land you in hot water if you live in a police state. All exiting traffic from your node (i.e. *other people's traffic*) is tied to your IP address and as others have found, you put yourself at risk by what others on the other side of the planet do with your node.

Lots of new Tor users fire up BitTorrent configured for Tor and suck down all the bandwidth. It makes for a very miserable Tor experience for other users. You may get served with a copyright violation notice (or sued), or perhaps raided if child porn flows out of your pipes. Think carefully and do your research before taking on such a risky charge, lest your computer be seized and your reputation ruined.

Running an Exit Relay From Home

RUNNING it from home is even worse then using cloud storage, and is infinitely dangerous in the USA and UK. If the law for whatever reason has an interest in your Tor traffic, your PC might be seized, yes, but that's only the start. In the UK, there is no 5th amendment protection against self-incrimination. A crusty old judge can give you two years just for not forking over the encryption keys (which if they had, they would not have bothered raiding at 6AM).

Use a host instead that supports Tor. There is Sealandhosting.org, for one. They accept Bitcoins and do not require any personal info, only an email. They offer Socks, Dedicated Servers, Tor Hosting and VPS as well as Domains.

We'll get into the nitty details later, but these are the Rules I've set for myself:

- Refrain from routing normal traffic through it
- Never do anything illegal (more later as it's a grey area)
- Never put sensitive files on it (financial info, love notes, court docs)
- Be as transparent as possible that I'm running an exit

Intelligence Agencies

THEY'VE DECLARED war on Tor and its stealth capabilities, no doubt about it. And though they will fight tooth and nail to convince you it is for your own good, really what it all comes down to isn't so much national security as it is national control: Control over you in that they know not what you're doing on Tor, nor why.

They don't like that.

It's quite pompous of them to spend so much money and waste so much time chasing you simply because they don't like you or your actions not being easily identifiable.

As you probably know, it's more costly to go after a high-value target. But they do not know if you are a high-value target or merely low-hanging fruit. As we've seen in the case of bored Harvard students, anyone can get into serious trouble if they go into Tor blind as a bat.

Even Eric Holder has publicly pointed out that Tor users are labeled as "non-US persons" until identified as citizens. It's beyond pompous. It's criminal and unconstitutional. It sounds as if they view ALL Tor users as high-value targets.

And by the time you are identified as such, they have acquired enough power to strip you as well as millions of other citizens of their rights to privacy and protection under the Fourth Amendment of the Constitution.

They do this using two methods:

The Quantum and FoxAcid System

HERE IS the gist of it:
  - Both systems depend on secret arrangements made with telcos
  - Both involve lulling the user into a false sense of security
  - Neither system can make changes to a LiveCD (Tails)
  - Both can be defeated by adhering to consistent security habits.

Defeating this requires a mindset of diligence. DO NOT procrastinate. Decide ahead of time to avoid risky behavior. We'll get to them all. A good, security mindset takes time and effort and commitment to develop but should be nurtured from the very beginning, which is why the RISKS are placed up front, ahead of even the installation chapter. Things tend to drag in the middle of a book like this, and are often forgotten.

Speaking of risk, if you wonder what truly keeps me up at night, it's this: What do other nations tell high-level CEOs and Intelligence agencies (Hong Kong, for instance)?

If the only thing I can trust is my dusty old 486 in my attic with Ultima 7 still installed atop my 28.8k dialup modem, then it's safe to assume *every* commercial entity is jeopardized by the NSA. And if that's true, if the NSA has to jump hoops to spy on us, how easy is it to infiltrate American-owned systems *overseas with our data on those systems?*

To that, if no corporation can keep their private info under wraps, then eventually the endgame may evolve into a Skynet grid similar to the Soviet-era East/West block in which CEOs have to choose east or west. But that's like trying to decide whether you want to be eaten by a grizzly bear or a lion.

So then, you now know the real risks. The main ones, anyway.

Every one of these risks can be minimized or outright defeated using knowledge that is in this book. The sad part is that most readers will forget roughly 80% of what they read. Those who take action will retain that 80% because they are making what they've read a reality: Making brilliant chess-like countermoves when the NSA threatens your Queen. If you do not take action ,but merely sit there like a frog in a slowly boiling pot of water, not only will *you* perish but your future generations will as well. Alright then. Enough of the risks. Let's get to it.

A FOOLPROOF GUIDE

Or As Foolproof As We Can Get It

NOW LET'S answer *what Tor is* and *what it does* and *what it cannot do*. You've no doubt heard it is some kind of hacker's tool, and you'd be right, but only from the perspective that a powerful tool like Tor can be used for just about anything. In fact anything can be bought (except maybe voluptuous blondes in red dresses) anonymously... as long as you're *cautious* about it.

Before you knock Tor, remember that it is not about buying drugs or porn or exotic white tiger cubs. It's about anonymous communication and privacy - with the main function being to grant you anonymity by routing your browsing session from one Tor relay to another--masking your IP address such that websites cannot know your real location.

This allows you to:

- Access blocked websites (Facebook if you are in China)
- Access .onion sites that are unreachable via the open internet

- Threaten the president with a pie-to-the-face...and no Secret Service visit!

It does all of this by a process called ***onion routing***.

Think of it as a multi-point-to-point proxy matrix. Unlike peer to peer applications like BitTorrent or eMule which expose your IP to everyone, Tor uses a series of intermediary nodes (and thus, IPs) that encrypt your data all along the network chain. At the endpoint, your data is decrypted by an exit node so that no one can pinpoint your location or tell which file came from which computer. Due to this anonymizing process, you are anonymous on account of the packed "onion layers" that hide your true IP address.

It is even possible to build a site such that only Tor users can access it. Also called "Onion Sites," though technically challenging, you don't need a Ph.D in computer science to build one. Or even a Bachelor's degree. These Onion sites are unaccessible by anyone using the regular web and regular, non-Tor Firefox.

We'll delve deeper into that later, as well as construct a fortress of doom that nothing can penetrate.

Installation

INSTALLING TOR IS DIRT SIMPLE. You can download it from the Tor website at:

https://www.torproject.org/download/download-easy.html.en

If your ISP blocks you from the Tor site, do this:

- Shoot an email to Tor. Tell them the situation. You can get an automated message sent back to you with the Tor installation package.

- Go to Google. Do a search for any cached websites, including Tor, that might have the install package to download. Many tech sites may just have it in the event of all-out nuclear war.

- Visit rt.torproject.org and ask them to mirror it.

- Get a friend to email you the Tor installation. Ask for Tails, too.

- VERIFY the signature if you obtain it elsewhere other than from the main Tor site, verify it even if your friend hand-delivers it. I've gotten viruses in the past from friend's sharing what they thought were "clean" apps.

Now then. Choose Windows, Linux or the Mac version and know that your default Firefox install will not be overwritten unless you want it to. Both use Firefox but Tor is a completely separate deal. You'll notice it has the same functions as Firefox: Tabs. Bookmarks. Search box. Menus. It's all here - except your favorite add-ons.

On that point, you might be tempted to install your favorites. Don't give in to that temptation. Multiple add-ons that do nothing for your anonymity might assist someone in locating you over Tor by what is known as "Browser fingerprinting."

NOW YOU'VE GOT some choices.

One is to volunteer your bandwidth, which makes it easier for other Tor users but comes with risk. More on that later but for now just know that every page you visit with the Tor Browser will be routed anonymously through the Tor network.

There is however an important detail you need to know concerning security, and that is that your Tor settings are merely reasonable *starting points*. They are not optimal. We're still at the infancy stage and quite frankly, optimal as Tor knows optimal is largely dependent on hardware (network, CPU, RAM, VM, VPN), and so each person's setup will be different.

WHAT TOR CANNOT DO

Now for what Tor *cannot* do, or at least cannot do very well. In the future this may change so don't fall on your sword just yet.

1.) TOR CANNOT PROTECT you from attachments.

THIS IS NOT LIMITED to executables but anything that can be run by way of code. This means Flash videos as well as RealPlayer and Quicktime, if you still use it. Those babies can be configured to send your real IP address to an adversary. Not good. So never run any executable or app unless you trust the source. If at all possible, go *open-source*. This also goes for any encryption scheme which you MUST use if you're going to use Tor. It is NOT an option. Some say it is but that's like saying learning Thai is optional if you're going to live in Bangkok. You won't get far that way.

2.) TOR CANNOT RUN torrents well.

OLD NEWS, right? Thousands still do this. Better safe than sorry, they claim. The only problem is they are safe and *everyone else* is sorry. Tor cannot do P2P apps like Emule and Limewire without making everyone else's Tor experience miserable. It simply sucks down too much bandwidth. In addition to some exit nodes blocking such traffic by default, it's been proven that an IP address can be found by using torrents over Tor. eMule, too, uses UDP and since Tor supports TCP protocol, you can draw your own conclusions about what that does to your anonymity.

True, you may be spared a copyright lawsuit since the RIAA likely won't go through all that trouble in trying to get your IP, but please spare other Tor users the madness of 1998 modem speeds. A VPN is a much better choice.

3.) TOR CANNOT CLOAK your identity if you are tossing your real email around like Mardi Gras beads. If you give your true email on websites while using Tor, consider your anonymity compromised. Your virtual identity must never match up with your real-life identity. Ever. Those who ignore this rule get hacked, robbed, arrested, or mauled by capped gremlins. Much more on this later.

FIVE

TOR APPS & ANTI-FINGERPRINT TOOLS

The Best of the Best

A few applications make Tor less of a headache, but they are not particularly well suited for desktop users unless you're doing some kind of emulation. But with everyone using mobile these days, some of these have benefited me in ways I never thought possible. Be sure and read the comments in the Play Store since updates tend to break things.

Orbot: Proxy with Tor

IT IS a proxy app that runs similar to the desktop app and encrypts your net traffic and protects you from surveillance and fortifies you against traffic analysis. You can use Orbot with Twitter, Duck-DuckGo or any app with a proxy feature. I've used this for a long time now and have gotten used to it. Perhaps it is time to try something else.

Invisibox - Privacy Made Easy

JUST PLUG the InvizBox into your existing router / modem. A new "InvizBox" wifi hotspot will appear. Connect to the new hotspot and follow the one time configuration set up and you're ready to go.

All devices that you connect to the InvizBox wifi will route their traffic over the Tor Network.

Text Secure

TEXTSECURE ENCRYPTS every message on your mobile phone and is simple to learn. Better still, in the event you leave your phone at Marble Slab (Marble Flab to the Mrs.), rest assured your privacy is safe due to encryption. It's also open-source. Far too many apps aren't, and thus cannot be peer-reviewed by, well, anyone, unlike some proprietary apps like those offered by SecurStar (i.e. Drive-crypt, Phonecrypt).

Red Phone

THIS APP SECURES every call with end-to-end encryption, allowing you privacy and peace of mind. It uses WiFi and offers neat upgrades if both callers have RedPhone installed.

It's not for everyone. Though it's not as expensive as say, Trust-Call, there are convenience issues like lengthy connection times and dropped calls (ever Skype someone from Manila?) so it's not going to be as quick and dirty as Jason Bourne does it.

But the pluses outweigh the minuses. I especially love the two-word passphrase as a security feature: If you fear Agent Boris is dead and has been killed by Agent Doris (who now has his phone), you can request she speak the second passphrase. Simple yet effective.

Google and Tor

WHAT DOES Google think of Tor? Quite honestly I suspect they try not to.

They probably don't *hate* it like the NSA does, but they know that if every Google user used Tor on a daily basis, much of their ad targeting system would, shall we say, begin firing *blanks*. Imagine if a thirteen year old boy received ads for Cialis, or an eighty-year old woman named Bertha began to see ads for Trojan coupons, or... well you get the idea.

They don't mind donating funds, either, since this allows a future stake in the technology (sort of). To that, they've not only donated to Tor, but to Freenet as well and even Mars rover technology. All kinds of crazy things. They never know which technology is going to rocket into orbit a week or year from now so they throw money around like Scrooge on Christmas morning.

Captchas

AT TIMES you'll be using Tor and find that Google spits this requirement out in order to prove you're human. This, on account of their massive analyses on search queries, is what drives some Tor users to think Google has it out for them.

However, Google has to put up with lots of spammers and general thievery; bots hammering the servers with tons of queries in short amounts of time that put undue strain on the servers can be one thing, but it can also happen if your employer uses proxies - many employees working for the same company that uses one of these can set off a red flag.

When your Tor circuit switches to a new one, usually it solves itself. There are other search engines like DuckDuckGo you can use, however.

You may find websites do the same thing. Again, this is on account of so many exit nodes (all of which are publicly visible to any website admin), slamming the website with traffic such that the hammering behavior resemble those of a bot, the kind Russian and Chinese outfits like to use.

SpiderOak

NORMALLY I WARN against using Cloud Service for anything you want private. SpiderOak one exception, with some reservation. It's a decent enough alternative to DropBox as it is coded with "Zero Knowledge" (so say the developer) and when you install it, a set of encryption keys is created client-side. When you upload data to SpiderOak servers, they're encrypted on *your* computer and *then* uploaded. Again, according to the developers.

They claim that even if a subpoena requires subscriber data, they could not deliver since only you have the keys. Not bad, but I still would not upload anything unencrypted. A container file, for instance.

The other downside is that it is centralized. Centralization means a single-point-of-failure. As well your data can be deleted by them at any time (true with any online service really). Remember that between you and a judge, they will always side with the judge.

SIX

TAILS

Ever heard of a "live system"? Neither had I until Tails burst on the scene. Tails allows you to use Tor and avoid tracking and censorship and in just about any location you could want. It houses its own operating system and is designed for those on the go.

You can run it via USB stick, SD or even a DVD. Pretty handy as this makes it resistant to viruses. It's also beneficial if you don't want your hard drive to leave remnants of your browsing session. The best part is that it's free and based on Linux *and* comes with chat client, email, office, and browser.

The downside to using a DVD is that you must burn it again each time you update Tails. Not very convenient. So let's install it to USB stick instead.

1.) Download the Tails installer at
https://tails.boum.org/install/win/usb/index.en.html
You must first install it somewhere, like a DVD, and then clone it the USB stick or SD card.

2.) Click Applications --> Tails --> Tails install to begin the installation.

3.) Choose Clone & Install to install to SD card or USB Memory Stick

4.) Plug in your device, then scan for the device in the Target-Device drop down menu. You'll get a warning about it overwriting anything on the device, blah-blah. Choose yes and confirm install.

Tails Limitations

NEITHER TAILS nor Tor encrypt your docs automatically. You must use GnuPG or LUKS for that (included), bearing in mind that some docs like Word or Atlantis may have your registration info within the document itself (In 2013, Amazon self-publishers discovered pen names could sometimes be revealed by looking at the code of the above apps and finding out the real identity of authors. Ouch.)

Personally I use fake info when "registering" any app I will use in conjunction with Tor or Tails.

OTHER NOTEWORTHY STUFF:

- Document metadata is not wiped with Tails

- Tails does not hide the fact you're using it from your ISP (unless you use Tor bridges). They cannot see what you're doing on Tor, true enough, but they know you're using it.

- Tails is blind to human error. Try not to use the same Tails session to begin two different projects. Use separate sessions. Isolating both identities in this way contributes to strong anonymity for your sessions.

Chrome

FIREFOX IS HARDLY the only way to slay a dragon. There's also Chrome. Yes, it's Google, and yes Google has strayed far from it's "Do

No Evil" motto, but like everything else in life, luck favors the prepared. You just have to have the right sword. The right armor. The right lockpicks. The preparations (reagents) are as follows:

I. INSTALL THE SCRIPTNO EXTENSION. It is to chrome what a mouse is for a PC, at least as far as precision aiming goes. It offers excellent control, too, even allowing you to fine-tune the browser in ways that NoScript for Firefox cannot. If you find it too difficult, ScriptSafe is another option. I've used both and came away very satis-fied, though like everything else on the internet, YMMV.

II. FlashControl is a nice alternative to Firefox. In the event you don't see it in the Google Play Store, just search for "Flash Block" and it should come up (Google has a habit of removing apps that aren't updated every Thursday under a Full Moon).

III. Adblock. This one is just insanely good at repelling all kinds of malware.

IV. User-agent Switcher for Chrome. Install it. Never leave home (0.0.0.0) without it. It spoofs and mimics user-agent strings. You can set yours to look like Internet Explorer. This will fool a lot of malware payloads into thinking you really are browsing with IE and not Firefox or Chrome, thus firing blanks at you.

IT MIGHT HAVE SAVED Blake Benthall, 26 year old operator of Silk Road 2.0, from getting raided by the FBI (among a dozen other drug outfits). This was accomplished over the span of many months since they had to get control of many relays, and if you have *control of relays*, you can use sophisticated traffic analysis to study patterns in IP addresses and match behavior and browser settings with those addresses. Recall that any federal prosecutor will always try to tie an IP address to an actual person where felonies are concerned.

It bears repeating.

An IP address is considered an *identity* for the purposes of prosecution.

We're all a number to them, regardless. Those of you with student loans know this perhaps more than anyone else. This will change as time goes on of course as Tor competitors like Freenet and other apps evolve to offer what Tor cannot. Ivan Pustogarov said the FBI did their homework and when all was said and done, had more resources on identifying lazy users than a typical VPN would.

V. CANVASBLOCKER - *And* another great plugin for Firefox. This prevents sites from using Javascript <canvas> API to fingerprint users. You can block it on every site or be discriminant and block only a few sites. Up to you. The biggest thing for me is that it doesn't *break* websites. More info here but in case you can't be bothered, here's the gist:

The different block modes are:

</canvas></canvas></canvas>

- block readout API: All websites not on the white list or black list can use the <canvas> API to display something on the page, but the readout API is not allowed to return values to the website.

- fake readout API: Canvas Blocker's default setting, and my favorite! All websites not on the white list or black list can use the <canvas> API to display something on the page, but the readout API is forced to return a new random value each time it is called.

- ask for readout API permission: All websites not on the white list or black list can use the <canvas> API to display something on the page, but the user will be asked if the website should be allowed to use the readout API each time it is called.

- block everything: Ignore all lists and block the <canvas> API on all websites.

- allow only white list: Only websites in the white list are allowed to use the <canvas> API.

- ask for permission: If a website is not listed on the white list or black list, the user will be asked if the website should be allowed to use the <canvas> API each time it is called.

- block only black list: Block the <canvas> API only for websites on the black list.

- allow everything: Ignore all lists and allow the <canvas> API on all websites.

As you can see, it's powerful stuff.

Firefox Armor

BUT FIRST A LITTLE mention of something a lot of people get wrong. You might be tempted to enable "Check for counterfeit websites" in Firefox. Don't do this as it will relay sites you regularly visit to Google's servers. Google's "predictive text-search" is also bad as it relays keystrokes to Google as well. To change it you have to do it manually by going into about:config in the address bar. That said, let's look at some other privacy settings you might want to know about.

Javascript - Avoid like the plague. You may notice it is turned on by default under the Firefox options tab, though. By the Tor Developer Team:

We configure NoScript to allow JavaScript by default in Tor Browser because many websites will not work with JavaScript disabled. Most users would give up on Tor entirely if a website they want to use requires JavaScript, because they would not know how to allow a website to use JavaScript (or that enabling JavaScript might make a website work).

There's a tradeoff here. On the one hand, we should leave Java-Script enabled by default so websites work the way users expect. On the other hand, we should disable JavaScript by default to better protect against browser vulnerabilities (not just a theoretical concern!). But there's a third issue: websites can easily determine whether you have allowed JavaScript for them, and if you disable Java-Script by default but then allow a few websites to run scripts (the way most people use NoScript), then your choice of whitelisted websites acts as a sort of cookie that makes you recognizable (and distinguish-able), thus harming your anonymity.

Ghostery and Ghostrank

NOT DEADLY, just useless on Tor since Tor disables tracking anyway. If you do use it, either could possibly alter your browser 'fin-gerprint', though not to the extent of breaking anonymity. Ghostery still blocks any tracking scripts regardless if you're on Tor or not. But use DuckDuckGo if you want to beef up your anonymity.

Adblock

THIS COULD ALSO CHANGE your fingerprint. Adblock plus has "acceptable ads" enabled by default, and there is also the scandals that Adblock has been in over the years, one implying that Google paid the Adblock CEO for Google Ads to be shown.

Besides, the basic idea of the Tor Browser Bundle is to use as few addons as possible. They figure that TorButton, NoScript, and HTTPS Everywhere is sufficient to preserve anonymity without the added risk of additional addons.

Whonix & Tor

IF YOU'RE paranoid that using Tor could get you into trouble (if you are hosting a Hidden Service), you might want to look into Whonix before running anything. Many power users who use Tor daily like the tighter security it offers. This is not to say that it is *better* than Tails by default. Both tools offer strengths and weaknesses meant for different purposes, and you may find one is better than the other for *your personal situation.*

Like Tails, Whonix is built with anonymity *and* security in mind. It's also based off of Debian/Linux, so it's a good synergy where anonymity is concerned. This synergy grants anonymity by routing everything through Tor. The advantages are that DNS leaks are next to impossible and malware cannot reveal your IP address. In fact, the only connections possible are routed through Tor via the Whonix-Gateway.

The question you may be wondering is: how much security is too much security? What's overkill and what isn't?

Well, you should ask how far will you fall if caught, and how much time are you willing to invest in reading to prevent it. Tails is easier to grasp, and if you do not expect attacks from sites you visit then by all means use Tails.

If you live in North Korea or China then there is a possibility of hard labor hammering worthless rocks if they see any Tor activity coming from your location that correlates to "things they don't like" activity... or anything else in the case of NK that offers hope. Guilty until proven innocent.

So if the above applies to you, use Whonix as it offers more security.

A few notable features of Whonix that make it more secure:

Anonymous Publishing/Anti-Censorship

Anonymous E-Mail w/Thunderbird or TorBirdy

Add proxy behind Tor (user -> Tor -> proxy)

Chat anonymously.

IP/DNS protocol leak protection.

Hide that you are using Tor

Hide the fact you are using Whonix

Mixmaster over Tor
Secure And Distributed Time Synchronization Mechanism
Security by Isolation
Send E-mail anonymously without registration
Torify any app
Torify Windows
Virtual Machine Images (VM)
VPN Support
Use Adobe Flash anonymously
Use Java/Javascript anonymously

THE FOLLOWING IS an example of a moderately secure system:

- Host Whonix on a memory stick with a flavor of Linux of your choice

- Use a VPN you trust (for privacy, not anonymity)

- Use Macchanger to spoof any mac address every session (Whonix does not hide your mac address from sites you visit!). If Macchanger isn't to your liking, give Technitium MAC Address Changer a try.

- Avoid regular calls of non-Tor WiFi tablets if using Cafe WiFi

- Know where every CCTV is located in the area you plan to use Tor

MAC Addresses

WE MENTIONED MAC ADDRESSES.

As technology would have it, your new WiFi/Ethernet card has something that can aid intelligence agencies in tracking you. It's a 48-bit identifier burned-in by the manufacturer. Sort of like an IMEI for your phone. If by chance you were not thinking clearly and bought your computer with Tor in mind using a credit card, you may later get targeted by an FBI "NIT" that swipes your MAC number. If that happens, you're toast.

The way to defeat this is to have a disposable MAC (the number, not the Apple product). One that you bought with cash with no security cams. That way you can get rid of it in a flash or swap it out.

They are also soft-configurable.

Believe it or not, Tails itself alters this randomly with every session. With a virtual machine, the FBI Nit may target a MAC number from the VirtualBox pool. Not really an issue unless they happen to raid your house and snag your system simultaneously. So swapping this out on a daily basis, as you've probably guessed, can be quite a pain. It's mainly for guys who run illegal markets. Guys who are *always* in the crosshairs of alphabet agencies.

But then, so can you. I've found it pays to think of oneself higher than what one is actually worth when traversing dark nets. Basically, thinking of yourself as a **high value target**. You'll subconsciously program yourself to research more, learn more, from everything from bad security mistakes to bad friendships to bad business practices. To that, you don't have to be in the top 5% of guys who've mastered network security. Being in the top 25% pool is more than enough to make The Man get frustrated enough to look for his flashy headlines elsewhere.

Whonix Bridges

IF YOU LIVE in a communist hellscape where even mentioning Tor can get you into trouble, using a Bridge with Whonix can be quite literally a life saver.

What Bridges Are

BRIDGES ARE obfuscation tools to cloak your Tor usage from a nosy ISP or government who might see you are using Tor, but not know what you are doing with it. To that end, Tor bridges are alternative ways to enter the Tor network. Some are private. Many are public. Some are listed on the Tor homepage. In a hostile environment you can see the value in using it to your advantage as it makes it *much more* difficult for an ISP to know you're using Tor.

What Bridges Are Not

WHILE NOT ESPECIALLY *UNRELIABLE,* they are certainly *less* reliable than regular Tor usage where performance goes. But the tradeoff may be in your best interest. Only you can decide if the performance hit is warranted. Here's how to do it in Whonix.

Bridges must be added manually since there is no auto-install method for Whonix, but it is not difficult. You simply must enter them into the proper directory:
/etc/tor/torrc.

IF YOU'RE USING a graphical Whonix-Gateway, then browse to:
Start   Menu   ->   Applications   ->   Settings   ->   /etc/tor/torrc.examples
To edit your torrc file (necessary for bridge adding), browse to:
Start Menu -> Applications -> Settings -> /etc/tor/torrc
Then add whatever bridge you copied from the Tor bridges page (or a private one if you have it). Then restart Tor for it to take effect.

SEVEN

TOR AND VPNS

There is a lot of confusion among beginners when it comes to VPN companies. They read one thing and see something else in the media that contradicts that one thing. The cold, hard truth about VPN companies is that a few want your patronage so badly that they're likely to bury the fine print on their web page where it is difficult to read. Believe me, that's fine print that can get you sent to the Big House if you're not careful. It really is a minefield where these companies are concerned.

For this reason, you need to decide whether you want privacy or anonymity. They are different beasts that require different setups. And not every VPN user uses Tor and not every Tor user uses a VPN service, but it is advantageous to combine two powerful tools; one that affords privacy (the VPN) and one anonymity (Tor). Like I said, two different beasts.

But for what it's worth, if you like this combo then find a VPN that offers 128 bit encryption and that does not store **activity logs**. That's the first rule of business.

And here's the part where the fine print comes in. Many VPN companies *claim* they do not log a thing... but will gladly offer your subscriber data on a silver platter if a subpoena demands it. Between Big Money and Your Freedom, money always wins. They will not go to jail for you, ever. So do your due diligence and research.

Obviously a VPN service is not anonymous by default. Providers love to tout that it is, but let's face it there is nothing anonymous about using someone else's line if you left a money trail leading straight to your front door.

Enter Tor, slayer of gremlins and we-know-what-is-better-for-you nanny staters. Tor makes for an extra and formidable layer of security in that the thieves will have to go an extra step to steal something from you. Thieves come in all flavors, from simple jewel thieves to border guards who want to make you as miserable as they are. So it is a good idea to ensure all the holes in your Tor installation are updated.

Updated applications are resistant to malware attacks since it takes time to find exploitable holes in the code. But... if you do not update then it does not matter which VPN you use with Tor since your session may be compromised. Here is what you can do:

Option 1

Pay for a VPN anonymously

THIS MEANS NO CREDIT CARDS. No verified phone calls. No links to you or anyone you know. In fact, leave no money trail to your real name or city or livelihood at all and never connect to the VPN without Tor.

For optimal anonymity, connect to your VPN through Tor using Tails. Even if the VPN logs every session, if you *always* use Tor with Tails, it would take an extremely well-funded adversary to crack that security chain. Without logging, it's even more secure.

But always assume they log.

OPTION **2**

Pay for a VPN using a credit card

CONNECTING with Tor when using a card with your name on it does nothing for anonymity. It's fine for privacy, but not for anonymity. This is good if you want to use Pandora in Canada for instance but not if you want to hire a contract killer to loosen Uncle Frick's lips a bit. Uncle Frick, who is 115 years of age and being tight-lipped on where the sunken treasure is.

Ahem, anyway, VPN services sometimes get a bad rap by anonymity enthusiasts, but signing up *anonymously* for a VPN has advantages. It strengthens the anonymity when using Tor, for one.

Even if the VPN keeps logs of every user, they will not know even with a court order the real identity of the user in question. Yet if you used Paypal, Bitcoin, credit cards or any other identifiable payment methods to subscribe to a VPN for the express purpose of using Tor, then anonymity is weakened since these leave a paper trail (Bitcoin by itself is not anonymous).

But the real down and dirty gutter downside is .onion sites. These are sites that can only be accessed by using Tor. The problem is that the last link of connectivity for these sites needs to be Tor, not the VPN. You'll understand what is involved once you connect with one which brings up our next question.

How Tor Friendly is the VPN?

THAT DEPENDS. Spammers use Tor. Hackers use Tor. Identity thieves use Tor. A few VPNs have reservations about letting users attain 100% anonymity by signing up anonymously. But if you signed up anonymously then you have little to fear since at that point it is *their* nose on the line.

There is one problem: the hardliners at the FBI do not like this attitude. In fact, they'd just as soon go after you if you use a VPN over Tor. Might a person come under twice the suspicion by using both? Maybe.

FROM FEE.ORG

"The investigative arm of the Department of Justice is attempting to short-circuit the legal checks of the Fourth Amendment by requesting a change in the Federal Rules of Criminal Procedure. These procedural rules dictate how law enforcement agencies must conduct criminal prosecutions, from investigation to trial. Any deviations from the rules can have serious consequences, including dismissal of a case. The specific rule the FBI is targeting outlines the terms for obtaining a search warrant.

IT'S CALLED Federal Rule 41(b), and the requested change would allow law enforcement to obtain a warrant to search electronic data without providing any specific details as long as the target computer location has been hidden through a technical tool like Tor or a virtual private network. It would also allow nonspecific search warrants where computers have been intentionally damaged (such as through botnets, but also through common malware and viruses) and are in five or more separate federal judicial districts. Furthermore, the provision would allow investigators to seize electronically stored information regardless of whether that information is stored inside or outside the court's jurisdiction.

The change may sound like a technical tweak, but it is a big leap from current procedure."

THE NSA DOES this without hindrance. We know this from Snowden's leaks that the FBI uses the NSA's metadata from private citizen's phone records. Thus, a VPN is not a truly formidable obstacle to them.

But this takes it to an entirely different level since if merely signing up for a VPN provides a basis for a legal search, then they can snoop on any ISP's server they want with no legal grounds at all to justify it. They've done similar things in Brazil.

But here in America, it usually goes down like this:

1.) Spy on JoBlo to see what he's up to.

2.) Make justification to seize PC/Raid/Data by reconstructing case

3.) Apply pressure to the right people with direct access to subscriber info

4.) Subpoena to decrypt subscriber's data. If they've done it once, they can do it a hundred more times. No Big Deal.

Solution

IF YOU'RE GOING to go the VPN route, then use PGP: Pretty Good Privacy. Never, ever transmit plain data over a VPN, not even one that offers SSL.

1.) Talking to police will never help you. Even in a raid situation. They wake you at gunpoint at 6AM and corral your family and threaten to take everyone to jail unless someone confesses. It's all lies, all the time by these agencies. A friend once remarked that a plain-clothes officer once knocked on his door to ask him if he was using Tor, only to *make sure he wasn't doing anything illegal.* He answered yes, but nothing illegal sir. That gave incentive to go forward like a giant lawnmower right over his reputation. He was proven innocent later on but not before the cops dragged that man's reputation through the mud. No public apology came (Do they ever?).

2.) If they don't charge you for running a hidden service, walk out. In fact, if they don't charge you with *anything*... walk out. Every word out of your mouth will aid them, not you.

3.) You have no reason to justify anything done in your own home to them, or anywhere else. The responsibility to prove guilt is theirs, not yours.

But, if you are in a situation where you have to talk or give up your encrypted laptop, always *always* give up your laptop first. Laptops are cheap and easy to replace. Five years is not.

USING **Bitcoins to Signup Anonymously to a VPN Service**

BITCOINS ARE NOT DESIGNED for absolute anonymity, but neither are VPNs. They're designed for privacy. So why use them?

Well because any extra layer that strengthens your anonymity is a layer you want. But just as with any advanced tool, you can lessen anonymity if you are careless with it. Good, tight anonymity tools can be a bane or a boon: A boon provided you do your homework. If not, folly and embarrassment ensues, possibly a situation where, depending on the country you're in, you might as well slap the cuffs on yourself. It's sad that the times have come to this predicament.

So let's consider then how one pays for a VPN and obtains this level of absolute anonymity - recognizing that a VPN by itself will do nothing to further this goal. It is only one tool in a toolbox full of tools and Bitcoin is only one of them as well. You wouldn't try to repair a Camaro engine with only a wrench, would you?

Now then, back to Bitcoin.

Bitcoins are open source coins, a digital currency that utilizes P2P-like code, and like *real* money you can buy online products with it. Products like memory cards at Newegg or even a Usenet or VPN premium service. These are useful to us. Using these Bitcoins, you the end-user, completely bypass the need for a credit union or bank. Pretty neat. But, they're not without their shortcomings.

For now simply know that they are created from the collective CPU computations of a matrix of users (like you, for instance) who donate to their creation. Bitcoin mining is involved, and though you may have seen images of Bitcoins on websites stamped with a golden "B", they are actually not something you can carry around in your pocket.

Not in the way you think at least.

They have something in common with PGP - public and private keys - just like the PGP application, only instead of verifying your identity like PGP does, Bitcoins verify your *balance*. This is where **Bitcoin wallets** come in. Again, not a magic bullet but rather one tool at our disposal.

On that point, Bitcoin Wallets will only get better at strengthening anonymity in the coming years. They will accomplish this by breaking the trail to our real identities. Oh, and their development is constantly improving.

However as we mentioned earlier--embarrassment will result if you neglect to do your homework, for every purchase by a particular wallet can be traced. That's right. If you buy a new video card at Newegg with it, the same that holds your credit card details, and then subscribe to a Usenet service or VPN, guess what... you've now established a trail to your real identity. The FBI or Chinese government will not need baying bloodhounds to sniff you out.

But not if you make only one purchase per wallet.

This means never using it for *any* online entity in which you've purchased goods while your real IP is connected. It also means forgoing Google Plus, Facebook, Skype and all social media outlets with said wallet. Twitter, Wal-Mart, BestBuy and even small mom & pop stores with multi-social media buttons splattered all over their websites--these are enemies of anonymity whether they know it or not (more likely they don't). They are not our friends anymore than a grenade is your friend after pulling the pin.

A single individual might hold several addresses and make only two purchases a year, but if he cross-contaminates by mixing up (each transaction is recorded in the Bitcoin blockchain), then anonymity is weakened and in most cases, destroyed by his own making. Not good.

The trick is this: don't create a pattern. A string of purchases create a pattern; the exact sort of pattern Google and Amazon code into their algorithms to search and better target you with interest-based ads. Bad for anonymity and that's far from the worse that can happen.

We get around this problem by using **Bitcoin mixers**. These weaken the links between several different Bitcoin addresses since the history of that purchase is wiped by the exchange of Bitcoins among other Bitcoin users.

Bitcoin Wallets

IN ORDER TO subscribe to a VPN or buy anything online with Bitcoins, a Bitcoin wallet is required. More than one type is available to us. We'll go through each and list their pros and cons.

Desktop Wallet

This is what I use and for good reason: I have absolute control over it not to mention the thought of having to access my money on someone else's web server defeats the entire idea of anonymity. I would never store my encrypted files "in the cloud" and neither should you. At least, not without an insanely secure system.

Think about it. Would you bury your safe in the neighbor's yard with a For Sale sign out front? Same deal. The server could go down. The company could go bankrupt. Any person on the other end on the hosting side can install a keylogger without your knowledge. Nasty buggers, those things. Desktop wallets aren't perfect, mind you, but they are better than The Cloud. One downside is that you must backup your Bitcoin wallet, an especially imperative task if it contains a lot of money. I do this quite religiously every week, as should you. Apologies if this all sounds like a Sunday sermon, but some of this stuff really must be taken as gospel.

Mobility/Travel Wallet

AS THE NAME IMPLIES, you carry this on you to make purchases in the same way you would a credit card. Convenience x 1000.

There are many types of wallets such as Coinbase and Electrum but I found Multibit to be very easy to learn. It is available in both Linux and Windows and offers a pass phrase option. Even the balance sheet looks like a PGP interface, but yet is beginner friendly and open-source, so no backdoors. Good for anonymity.

MULTIBIT WINDOWS INSTALL

NOW WE COME to the instructions for a clean install of this work of wonder.

DOWNLOAD THE INSTALLER.

The possible problems we may run into: On Windows 7 64-bit which is the system of choice outside of Linux these days, it may be that the Java Virtual Machine (JVM) is not correctly located, or "Failed to create a selector" is shown in the error message. A solution is to change the compatibility setting:

Choose the compatibility dialog (right click--> icon - Properties --> Compatibility)

Choose: "Run this program in compatibility mode for Windows XP SP3."

Check the box: "Run this program as an administrator"

Multibit Linux Install

IF YOU'RE a Linux fan (and you should be if anonymity is something you strive for), then download the Linux / Unix installer here:

https://multibit.org/help/v0.5/help_installing.html

Open a terminal window and create an installer executable with:

CHMOD +X multibit-0.5.18-linux.jar

RUN THE INSTALLER: java -jar multibit-0.5.18-linux.jar

INSTALL.

THEREAFTER YOU WILL HAVE a shortcut to start MultiBit in your "Applications | Other" menu. If you see no MultiBit shortcut, you can run MultiBit manually by doing the following:

Open a terminal window and 'cd' to your installation directory

type java -jar multibit-exe.jar

NOW IT IS time to purchase Bitcoins. There are several options but what we want to do is execute an offline option; to buy Bitcoins *off the grid* which cannot be traced. Cash n' carry.

LocalBitcoins look promising as does TradeBitcoin. But as Trade looks down so let's go with LocalBitcoins.

- After you choose a Bitcoin outfit, you must signup for the site (anonymously) but be aware of the interest charges which vary from one to another depending on how much you want to deal in. For this transaction, use an email in which you anonymously signed up. That means:

- Tor Browser/Tails

- No Facebook or other Social Media/Search cookies present on machine

- Only accessed for Tor/Bitcoins.

CHOOSE 'PURCHASE' on the seller's page and the amount we wish to buy. Remember, we're not buying a house here, only a VPN to use with Tor. Once funds are transferred out of escrow, you will be notified.

Notice that the trader you are dealing with might be able to see your financial information, i.e. which bank you use, etc., but you can always opt to meet up in person if you want. This carries a whole other set of risks.

Check to make sure the funds are in your Bitcoin Wallet.

Paying for a VPN to Use with Tor

NOW IT IS time to pay for your VPN service... *anonymously*. Let's choose Air VPN at $9/mo and who also accepts Bitcoins for payment.

First: Sign up for the service but do not put any information that you've used on any other site such as usernames or passwords. Also, since we do not need to input any banking info, no money trail will be traced to us. The email we use is a throwaway email (you did use Tor to signup, right?)

Second: Give them the wallet address for our Bitcoin payment. Hit send.

Done!

Like any Usenet service, a VPN service will send confirmation to your email with details you need to use that service. Afterward you can see the details of this payment in your Bitcoin wallet.

As you can see, a Ph.D in Computer Science is not needed for this extra layer of anonymity. The problem with the mass of people on Tor, however, is that they cannot be bothered to do these simple extra steps. That's bad for them. Good for you. Those that wear extra armor are often the ones left standing after a long battle. But there is one topic left to discuss, and it's the most important:

EIGHT

REAL IDENTITIES OUTSIDE OF TOR

This is a big one.

One that I'm guilty of breaking because even anonymity nuts can crack under peer pressure every now and then and do something dumb like use Facebook over Tor (my early days, thankfully). A question I kept asking back then was this:

What kind of danger is there in using your real name online?

It depends.

Law enforcement and prospective employers who mine your social media presence for data are often worse than thieves who salivate when you announce on Twitter you'll be out of town for two weeks. Thieves, while unsavory and criminally deviant to be sure, rarely profess to be just. And thieves, as stated before, come in all shapes and sizes. If they take your private data without asking you first, that's stealing.

Employers can be the worst of the lot, as hypocritical as Harvey Two-Face, demanding transparency in *your* life but not their *own*. Make an inflamed political post or drink wine on vacation in Bora Bora with Filipinas twirling fire sticks and you could lose your job, or be *denied* one. Not kidding. Mention you use Tor and you may hear your interviewer ask:

"I noticed you're a big fan of Tor. Could you elaborate on why you need to use an anonymizing service? We like transparency in our employees."

Yes, I was actually asked this in an interview for a position that handled a lot of money. It came out of nowhere, but what really bothered me was the casual way it was asked, like every applicant should have something to hide if they desire anonymous communications. Maybe I was some rabid fan of Jason Bourne and up to no good. At any rate, they did not like my answer.

"Because I value freedom."

I came out of that interview perplexed, yet jobless, viewing privacy as somewhat of a double-edged sword since one *needs* an online presence for many higher paying employers. It did not sit well with me. I felt a little cheated to be honest and as I drove home, some of the mumblings I overheard later on became as loud as roaring trains in my ears:

Don't like someone on Facebook? You probably won't like working with them.

Like the competitor's products? Here's our three-year non-compete agreement for you to sign.

You use Tor? The only people that use that are terrorists, pedos and hitmen.

Soon thereafter, any time a prospective employer noticed "Tor" under the Hobbies section of my resume, it would always illicit a negative reaction. My breathing would become erratic as my heart raced, as if they were about to summon an unbadged "authority" to warn me of being *too private*.

He would dress a lot like Dilbert, only he'd be skinnier, and with a bumblebee-yellow pen and a clipboard. He'd have multiple facial tics and a quirky habit of raising a Vulcan eyebrow as if it were purely illogical to value privacy. I have no idea why he'd have a clipboard, but he always did.

My solution was to rightly divide my public and private identity in social settings and remove any trace of it on my resume. In fact, I did not give any indication on any social media site, either, that I was into any of the following:

- PGP
- Encryption, or encrypting files or Operating Systems
- Tor Relays
- I₂P
- Freenet
- Anonymity in general
- *Anything* linking to Edward Snowden

Such is the nature of the masses. One simply cannot rely on Facebook or Twitter or Google to respect one's freedom to use Tor without announcing it to the whole world.

But with Tor, Google cannot mine your browsing session for ads. No ads = no soup for them. From NBC:

"The Internet search giant is changing its terms of service starting Nov. 11. Your reviews of restaurants, shops and products, as well as songs and other content bought on the Google Play store could show up in ads that are displayed to your friends, connections and the broader public when they search on Google. The company calls that feature "shared endorsements."

So I firewall everything I do. I use Ghostery for social sites and offer only pseudonymous details about myself. In fact, I try to avoid any correlation between Tor and any social media site just as one would a can of gasoline and a lighted match.

Anonymous Bullies

THE MEDIA along with Google and Facebook seems to think that if only everyone's name were known to them, then every bully from California to Florida would go up in smoke.

Vampirism, like bullying, comes in many forms, but if you've ever read Anne Rice then you know every clan is as different as diamonds are to lumps of coal. But they do usually share similar *beginnings*. Take adolescence for example.

Were you ever bullied in school? I was. I remember every buck toothed spiked-club wielding ogre who pelted me into nothing but a wet snowball in 7th grade, and it didn't stop there. How I wished it had, but not having Aladdin's lamp made things difficult. I watched as they spread like cancer, sludging upward to other grades for easier victims. Ninth on upward to 12th and even into the workforce. Bullies who'd make great orc chieftains if there were any openings, such was their cruelty and ire.

I recall one particularly nasty breed of ogre in 8th grade. He was the worst of the lot. A walking colossus who sweat when he ate as though he were being taken over by something in The Thing. Either that or Mordor. He certainly had the arms for it. When he arced an arm over me it sounded like a double-bladed axe slicing the air in half.

Harassment grew more fierce and fiery every year. Later I would learn that his entire family, perhaps his entire *generation*, grew up being the baddest of the bad - bullies that thrived on terrorizing to make a name for themselves. Every one of them went on to become cops in the New Orleans area. One died of diabetes. Another went on to join the ATF to fight the evil scourge called *drugs* (how'd that work out?).

I knew everything about these cretins and not just their names. I knew who their parents were. What they did for a living. Who they hung out with. What beers their dad's drank and with what porn mags. Gossip spread like wildfire in high school and no detail of identifying information was ever left out.

And yes, I told the principle, a great big lady named Beverly whose former job was working in some HR high-rise. I remember multiple times meeting her in that office where glitzy awards hung like a safari hunter's office and thinking if only she had an elephant gun I could borrow. Boom! My trouble's be over (so thought the 13 year old).

Meetings between my circus acrobat mother became fruitless and rather embarrassing. Absolutely nothing positive came of it. The point, however, isn't that nothing came of it, but that nothing came of it even as I knew **everything** about the scourge I faced daily. Knowing their identities did, well, not much of anything. Knowing their names did nothing. Knowing how many other kids they tormented did nothing and, let's face it, kids just aren't smart enough to band together and attack no matter how many times we watched Road Warrior.

We can see how bullying spreads on Facebook. Like anthrax. Little wolves ostracize a rejected member when a drop of fear is shown, so they crucify without knowing much of anything about him or why he's being targeted. Real names? Check. Real addresses? Yep. Everything is traceable now just as it was way back then. And still the orcs come in a blood-toothed frenzy like sharks to a wounded dolphin.

When 13 year olds begin hanging themselves in mom's bedroom to escape the torture, one thing is immediately obvious: what they really want is to *disappear*. They want *anonymity*.

But that's not something bullies think highly of. They won't allow it. Neither do they allow running away, not that a kid has the means anyway: No money. No car. No distant relatives in Alaska to run and live with and hunt moose all winter.

Anonymity is not an option. It's a requirement. It should be the law on some level but isn't. This is because if they gave us true anonymity, they would lose the precious power they wield over us. If Google and Facebook ever teamed up with the federal government to require ID to access the internet, we'd all be better off going face-to-face with an Alaskan grizzly.

<u>Email Anonymity</u>

THERE WAS a time when we didn't have to worry about what we said in emails. Security? That was something geeks did. Geeks and supergeeks who attended hacker conventions and scoured Usenet for zero-day exploits. It was the days of Altavista and Infoseek, when Google was still wet behind the ears and Microsoft was still struggling to satisfy every Dos user's whim. We wrote whatever we wanted and hit send with nary a worry about third parties intercepting it and using our own words against us. Sadly, no longer.

Advertising and search engines now tailor advertisements to individuals based on what you like and are sure to click. Trails are left. Messages are scanned. And Gmail is no different than Yahoo or Microsoft. In fact, judges wield more power with the pen than any CEO in any company in North America.

When a trailer is leaked or someone says something nasty about the government, you can bet IP addresses will be subpoenaed. Sometimes I imagine a lot of ex-Soviet officers are laughing at how many snitches the Internet produces on a yearly basis. Subversion to the extreme.

But is it possible to send a message that is *foolproof* against subpoenas?

There are, in fact, many flavors to choose from to accomplish this task. Below are a few rock-solid services. Combined with Tor, they grant you a virtual fortress. Anonymity squared if your message is encrypted.

The first is <u>TorGuard</u>.

TorGuard allows users to use PGP (Pretty Good Privacy) in email so you needn't worry about snooping. You get 10MB plus several layers of protection with mobility support.

SECOND IS <u>W3, The Anonymous Remailer</u>
Connectable with Tor, you only need an email address to send

the message to (preferably encrypted with PGP--more on that in a moment).

Another is Guerrilla Mail. They allow users to create throwaway emails to be used at leisure. Emails sent are immediately wiped from the system after you hit Send. Well, within one hour at any rate.

ALL OF THESE services claims of anonymity would be pretty thin if we did not encrypt our messages-- which brings us to PGP.

PGP is the encryption standard of choice for many old users like myself, and for good reason. It has never been cracked by the NSA or FBI or any intelligence agency and likely won't until quantum computers become common. It works by way of key pairs, one which is public and one private (the one you will use to decrypt your messages with).

Worry not about the term "keys". It is not difficult to grasp and will be as easy as hitting send once you've done it a few times.

The first thing you must do is make your public key available. This is only used to verify your identity and is not the same as divulging your passphrase for say, a Drivecrypt container. Your recipient must also share with you their key so you can respond in turn.

The good news?

Only the two of you will be able to read each other's messages. The caveat is if the other person is compromised and you don't know about it. They will read everything you encrypt. Here is what you need to know:

1.) To begin, make two keys, one public--for everyone else but you--and one that you wouldn't even share with your own mother. You should back this key up in a secure medium, and remember that if it isn't backed up to three different types of media, it isn't backed up. If your truly paranoid, send one on an encrypted microSD to your parents in case of housefire. Yes, it does happen.

2.) IF HOWEVER YOU opt to tell mom, then she will need your public key (you did publish it on a <u>public key server</u>, right?) Then you can read it by way of your private key. She doesn't know this key (thank the gods!)

3.) YOU CAN "SIGN" any message you want over Tor or anywhere else (Freenet, for example, the highest security setting of which demands absolute trust of your friend's darknet connection) to verify it is really you sending it.

UNLESS NORMAN BATES does a shower scene on you and takes your keys. Your mom can then verify with your public key that it is really you.

4.) USERS you've messaged with (or not) can sign your public key as a way of verifying your identity. As you can see, the more people that do this, that is, *vouch for you*, the better.

<u>Important</u>

UNLESS YOU'VE GOT the photographic memory of Dustin Hoffman in Rainman, it's a good idea to store your public/private keys and passwords and also revocation-certificate to backup media so you can retrieve it five years down the line... should you need it. And believe me, you will!

Encrypt them in containers. Always print your key-file or pass phrase and deposit in a safe place. If you lose it, all documents encrypted with it are permanently lost. There are no back-doors and no way to decrypt without it. Also, consider making an expiration date at key-pair creation.

If you like nice and easy interfaces, try Mymail-Crypt for Google's Gmail. It is a plugin that allows users to use PGP-encrypted messages in a handy interface, though ensure your browser is air-tight secure and you trust it with your private key.

One More Thing

RATHER THAN HAVING to encrypt files and upload them somewhere unsafe, look at AxCrypt encryption tool. This is useful if you're used to uploading to Dropbox or Google Drive. Just remember that in the event you upload an encrypted file to "The Cloud," you will not know it if your password to said file has been compromised without setting strict security rules.

With that said, let's configure PGP for Windows

- Install Gpg4Win

- Next, create your key in Kleopatra and choose Export-Certificate-to-Server by right click so you can publish it to a keyserver. Get a trusted friend to "sign" and establish trust.

- Use Claws-Mail client that comes packaged with it or use Enigmail if you're using Thunderbird.

- Send a few messages back and forth to your trusted friend via PGP to get the hang of things.

- Optionally you can set a Yahoo/Gmail/Hotmail filter so as to forward any messages that contain "Begin PGP message" to a more private account.

Tor Instant Messaging Bundle

IT IS no secret that the NSA has Skype, Yahoo Chat and other instant message services in their hands, but as long as the Tor development team knows about it, they can do something about it.

Enter Tor Instant Messaging Bundle.

True anonymity is the goal of this application. It is built by the very same who developed the Tor browser bundle and like that application, will route all communication through Tor relays... encrypted *backwards and forwards* and hidden from the NSA's prying eyes.

There is also Torchat.

Torchat, like Yahoo's IM, offers encrypted chat and even file-sharing. Since it is built upon Tor, you are assured absolute privacy on what you say and to whom you say it. Both Windows and Mac versions are available and no install is necessary. Just unzip anywhere and run (preferably from an encrypted hard drive or USB-Drive) the blue earth symbol titled 'Torchat'.

A few more useful apps:

ChatSecure - ChatSecure is mainly used for encrypted messaging on mobility devices but they offer PC, Linux and Mac versions as well. From their website:

THE GUARDIAN PROJECT creates easy to use secure apps, open-source software libraries, and customized mobile devices that can be used around the world by any person looking to protect their communications and personal data from unjust intrusion, interception and monitoring.

Whether your are an average citizen looking to affirm your rights or an activist, journalist or humanitarian organization looking to safeguard your work in this age of perilous global communication, we can help address the threats you face.

TELEGRAM - THIS APP also focuses on messaging but with superior speed and is similar to SMS and allows for picture/video sending. There are also 'Secret Chats' that offer encrypted sessions. They claim no data is kept on their servers and you can even set the app to permanently delete all messages.

CryptoCat - Billed as an alternative to social media chat apps like those seen on Facebook, Twitter and the like, CryptoCat gives you encrypted communications using the AES encryption standard. All encrypted info is deleted after an hour of inactivity.

Freenet - This is the granddaddy of all anonymous systems the world over, both for file sharing or any kind of secret chats. Explaining everything it has to offer goes far beyond our Tor discussion as they are two different systems, but I include it here as an alternative if you find Tor lacking.

And it is not as simple as Tor, nor is it as fast unless you leave it running 24/7. It is not for everyone as there are all manner of criminal entities that use it and you will notice this if you load up any groups. It is hard to ignore and unlike Usenet, there is no one to file a complaint with. No one to report. It is anarchy multiplied many times over in many groups, but there are ways of mitigating the damage.

But for *absolute anonymity* and freedom of speech, there is no better tool to use if you have the patience to learn its darknet offerings.

FROM THE WEBSITE:

Freenet is free software which lets you anonymously share files, browse and publish "freesites" (web sites accessible only through Freenet) and chat on forums, without fear of censorship. Freenet is decentralised to make it less vulnerable to attack, and if used in "darknet" mode, where users only connect to their friends, is very difficult to detect.

Communications by Freenet nodes are encrypted and are routed through other nodes to make it extremely difficult to determine who is requesting the information and what its content is.

Users contribute to the network by giving bandwidth and a portion of their hard drive (called the "data store") for storing files. Files are automatically kept or deleted depending on how popular they are, with the least popular being discarded to make way for newer or more popular content. Files are encrypted, so generally the user cannot easily discover what is in his datastore, and hopefully can't be held accountable for it. Chat forums, websites, and search functionality, are all built on top of this distributed data store.

An important recent development, which very few other networks have, is the "darknet": By only connecting to people they trust, users can greatly reduce their vulnerability, and yet still connect to a global network through their friends' friends' friends and so on. This enables people to use Freenet even in places where Freenet may be illegal, makes it very difficult for governments to block it, and does not rely on tunneling to the "free world".

It is not as simple as using a Usenet provider's newsgroup reader. No sir, Freenet requires patience. Using Frost or Fuqid (Front End apps for the main Freenet program), it might be half an hour before you can "subscribe" to groups or download in the way you can Usenet. Some groups, like the Freenet group and other technical groups will be immediately available, but with few messages. Time will solve this. So keep it running in the closet and forget about it for a day or so if you plan on subscribing to a lot of groups.

It will be worth the wait.

Frost & Fuqid

THE TWO FREE front ends I recommend are: Frost and Fuqid.

Frost has seen a lot of improvements but I recommend you try Fuqid first as it is the first external app for Freenet that acts as as an insert/download manager for files. Fuqid stands for: Freenet Utility for Queued Inserts and Downloads and runs on Windows or Linux under wine.

The Fuqid freesite is on Freenet itself at:

USK@LESBxzEDERhGWQHl1t1av7CvZY9SZKGbCns-D7txqXoI,nPoCHuKvlbVzcrnz79TEd22E56IbKj-KHB-W8HHi9dM,AQACAAE/Fuqid/-1/

You will need to paste the above into Freenet's front control panel where it says "Key". It can take several minutes to load if you're new to the system.

After you've installed it, right click on the left side with your list of boards and choose "Add new board". For the name put in "fuqid-announce" with out the quotes. You will now find a new board called "fuqid-announce" in your list of boards.

Right click this board and choose "Configure selected board". This will bring up a new window. On that window click "Secure board" to change it from a public board. Now in the section that says "Public key" paste in the key below:

SSK@qoY-E5SKRu66pmKH64xa~R~w3hXmS5ZNtqnpE-GoCVww,HTVcdWChaaebfRAublHSxBSRaRFG91qCwsa3m-GF3-QE,AQACAAE

Now you have the announce board for Fuqid added to your Frost boards. The latest releases of Fuqid will be posted to this board along with the fuqid board on FMS. Questions? Direct them to the Frost or FMS board called Fuqid.

Passwords

GOOD, strong passwords are like having a couple of Rottweilers sleeping in your den. Most intruders will leave when the chaos starts. Weak passwords are like having a Golden Retriever. Nice and friendly and easy to trust around kids, but might just let out a little woof at 3AM when said intruder comes. Then he will hide under the coffee table (the dog, not the intruder).

I've heard for years that you should never use anything personal as your password. That includes family names. Favorite books. Movies. So what's the solution?

Remix your passwords with a symbol or two. If you think a hacker won't be able to guess the name of your girlfriend's locker combination, you'd be mistaken. It is dirt simple to guess even if you mix it up a bit. Computers devoted to this practice can guess many in less than a nanosecond.

BUT HOW DO you remember a password for a site used over Tor that has symbols?

Easy. Use a passphrase that is simple to recall for you only. First write out the first letter of each word, taking not of case and position. Insert symbols therein. For instance:

LAST SUNDAY, the wife bought me a Rolex watch and it was too ugly. Which when changed is:

LS,twbmarwaiw2u

The above pass is hard for a hacker to guess but easy for you to remember... assuming you are good at substitution.

Changing Your Passwords

PROVIDED you've followed the above to the letter, you shouldn't have to rotate out your passwords every 90 days. I'm sure you've heard from both sides of the aisle their say on the subject, but I believe research has proven that keeping a strong password (unless proof of compromise) is a safe bet.

THE RESEARCH PAPER FROM ACM/CCS 2010: "The Security of Modern Password Expiration: An Algorithmic Framework and Empirical Analysis" by Yinqian Zhang, Fabian Monrose and Michael Reiter came to the conclusion that changing passwords every few months did not, repeat, did NOT increase security:

at least 41% of passwords can be broken offline from previous passwords for the same accounts in a matter of seconds, and five *online password guesses in expectation suffices to break 17% of accounts.*

...our evidence suggests it may be appropriate to do away with password expiration altogether, perhaps as a concession while requiring users to invest the effort to select a significantly stronger password than they would otherwise (e.g., a much longer passphrase).

....

In the longer term, we believe our study supports the conclusion that simple password-based authentication should be abandoned outright.

Storing Passwords in Tor Browser

YOU MAY HAVE NOTICED that the "Remember Password" option in Tor Browser is not available, or so it seems. But if you look at the privacy setting and alter the history setting to "remember history" and "remember passwords for sites," it will no longer be greyed out.

Diceware

IF YOU MUST STORE PASSWORDS, a good option for a unique random one is Diceware - where you can get an expire date for any password months from the date of creation. You can copy any password to a text file then encrypt it and mail it to yourself or place on a removable (encrypted) drive or USB stick.

Remember: Tor does nothing to improve the security of your *system* to everyday attacks. It only improves security online, and even then only when used responsibly. Tor has no idea if your version of Windows is unpatched and infected with a zero-day malware payload that infected it with a keylogger.

One way in which a hacker could guess your complex password is if they linked your Tor usage with non-Tor usage and compromised your passwords from a non-Tor site. This is why you should never use the same usernames/passwords for Tor that you do for non-Tor activity.

PREVENTING **Non-Tor Activity From Being Linked with Tor Activity**

IT IS risky to browse different websites simultaneously and preserve anonymity since Tor might end up sending requests for each site over the same circuit, and the exit node may see the correlation.

It is better to browse one site at a time and thereafter, choose "New Identity" from the Tor button. Any previous circuits are not used for the new session.

Further, if you want to isolate two different apps (allow actions executed by one app to be isolated from actions of another), you can allow them to use the same SOCKS port but change the user/pass.

Another option is to set an "isolation flag" for the SOCKS port. The Tor manual has suggestions for this but it will lead to lower performance over Tor. Personally I like to use Whonix. Two instances, two VMs. One of them runs Tor and the other with Tor Firefox.

Keyloggers

YOU MIGHT WONDER what a keylogger has to do with Tor. Or for that matter, what a keylogger even is. You're not alone. In fact you'd be surprised how many people don't know and shocked how many techs consider them a non-issue.

In 2010 I caught up with an old childhood friend of mine I had not seen in over a decade. He was now an ATF agent. I was surprised and (falsely) assumed his extensive training meant he knew as much as an NSA agent when it came to computer security. Wrongo.

He replied to a post I made on a Facebook regarding the hacking group "Anonymous."

"What's a keylogger?" he asked. I waited for someone else to reply. No one did so I told him. He seemed amazed, dumbfounded, as though it were something only recently unleashed upon the net. I then told him that they had been around a long time.

But (sigh), there's a lot of confusion on what they do exactly. Some people call them spyware. Others say they're trojans. Still others, exploits. They're a little bit of everything to be honest.

They are *surveillance* software that tracks and records every click you make, every website visited, every keystroke typed. Chats, Skype, Emails. If you can type it, it can record it and all right under your very nose. It can even email what you type to a recipient on the other side of the world. CC numbers, passwords and Paypal login details are just the short list of targets it can acquire.

So how does one get in infected?

- Opening an email attachment
- Running an .exe file from a P2P network from an untrusted user
- Accessing an infected website with an outdated browser
- The NSA, if they can grease the right palms

Some employers use them to track productivity of employees. Some wives attach one via USB (Hardware version) to see who their hubbies are conversing with at night after bed. Parents use them on the kid's computer. So it isn't like they're 100% malicious *all the time*.

But they are devilishly difficult to detect. They wield an almost vampiric presence, but like vampires there are subtle signs you can glean without whipping out a wooden stake.

Vampire Signs

- SLUGGISH BROWSING SPEED

- Laggy mouse/pausing keystrokes in a text doc
- Letters don't match on display with what you type
- Errors on multiple webpages when loading heavy text/graphics

There are two types: software and hardware.

Software Keyloggers

THIS TYPE HIDES inside your operating system. They *lurrrve* Windows. Linux, not so much. The keylogger records keystrokes and sends them to a hacker or other mischief maker at set times provided the computer is online. Cloaked, most users will never see it working its dark art. Many popular anti-virus vendors have trouble identifying it because the definitions change so frequently.

Hardware Keyloggers

BOND MIGHT HAVE USED one of these. Being hardware, it is a physical extension that can plug into any USB on a PC and can be bought online by suspecting spouses or kids wanting access to their dad's porn stash. Keystrokes are logged to ram memory. No install needed.

Thus, unless you're the type to check your PC innards every day, you might not spot it until it's too late. They also can be built right into the keyboard. The FBI loves swapping the target's out with a carbon copy custom-built surveillance device. Granted, this is mainly for high-value targets like the Mafia but they're available to anyone.

Keylogger Prevention

- CHECK YOUR KEYBOARD for suspicious attachments. If you are an employee at X company and a new keyboard arrives at your desk one morning, exercise caution unless you trust your boss 200%.

- Use a Virtual Keyboard. No keystrokes = no logging!

- Use Guarded ID to prevent hackers from capturing your keystrokes. It works by scrambling everything you type, rendering any info useless to hackers.

- Use a decent firewall to stop a keylogger from delivering your data. A year ago, my Comodo firewall alerted me to suspicious network activity seemingly out of nowhere when I wasn't doing anything online. Turns out I had the Win64/Alureon trojan. I had to use Malwarebytes to detect and remove it. Norton was useless!

NINE

DARKNET MARKETS

Just how safe is a Darknet in light of the vulnerabilities discussed? The short answer is, *as safe as you make it.*

You are the weak link. The last link in the security chain. And although you need Tor to access Onion sites, the term can apply to any anonymous network - networks like I2P or Freenet or anything else that cloaks the source of data transmit, and by extension, your identity.

Which brings us to the *Darknet Marketplace.*

The complete list of such marketplaces on the deep web are numerous, and the risk of getting scammed is quite high. It's one reason why you may not have heard about them. They are often taken down quickly by either a venomous reputation or a law enforcement bust. Sometimes they piss off the wrong people and then spammers ddos the site. But there are numerous places one can go if you're curious about what is sold by whom.

When I say *sold*, what I mean is, anything you want that cannot be gained through the usual legal channels. And remember that what is legal in one country may be illegal in another. In Canada, lolicon comics are illegal and can get you in big trouble if you cross the border. But not in America. In the USA you can pretty much write any story you want. In Canada? TEXT stories involving minors are verboten.

The other difference is that there are safety nets in buying almost anything in a first world country on the open market. Think BestBuy. Mom and Pop stores. Florist shops. If customers get injured, what happens? Customers sue via the legal safety net and make a lot of lawyers a lot of money.

But the Darknet Marketplace laughs at any such safety nets. In fact, you're likely to get scammed at least a few times before finding a reputable dealer for whatever goods you seek. And it really doesn't matter what it is, either - Teleportation devices? Pets? Exotic trees? It's all the same that goes around. Whatever is in demand will attract unsavory types and not just on the buyer's end.

Therefore, research any darknet market with Tor, being careful to visit forums and check updated information to see if any sites have been flagged as suspicious or compromised. Some other advice:

- Always use PGP to communicate.

- Never store crypto-currency at any such marketplace.

- Assume a den of thieves unless proven otherwise by *them*. The responsibility is theirs just as it is offline, to prove they are an honest business. If you open your own, keep this in mind: customers owe you nothing. You can only betray them once.

Now for some examples of Phishers and Scammers and other Con men. By their fruits, ye shall know them.

1.) SILK ROAD 2.0 (E5WVYMNX6BX5EUVY...) Lots of scams with this one. Much like Facebook and Google emails, you can tell a fake sometimes by the address. Paste the first few letters into a shortcut next to the name. If it doesn't match, steer clear.

2.) **Green Notes Counter** (67yjqewxrd2ewbtp...)

They promised counterfeit money to their customers but refuse escrow. A dead giveaway.

3.) IPHONES FOR HALF OFF: (iphoneavzhwkqmap...)

Now here is a prime example of a scam. Any website which sells electronic gadgets on the deep web is ripe for scamming customers. Whereas in the Far East you will merely get counterfeit phones with cheap, Chinese made parts that break within a month, on the Deep Web they will simply take your money and say adios. Actually, they won't even bother saying that.

So then, how does one tell a scam?

Because many new darknet vendors will arise out of thin air, with rare products that will make customers swoon and send them money - without doing any research on their name or previous sales. A real hit and run operation. Hit quick and fast and dirty. Seduce as many as they can before the herd catches on to the wolf in disguise. Many are suckered, thinking "it's only a little money, but a little money from a lot of Tor users goes a long way in encouraging other scammers to set up shop.

When you ask them why they do not offer escrow, they say "We think it is unreliable/suspicious/unstable" amid other BS excuses. It is better to hold on to your small change than leave a trail to your treasure chest. And make no mistake some of these scammers are like bloodhounds where identity theft is concerned.

Do your research! Check forums and especially the dates of reviews they have. Do you notice patterns? Are good reviews scattered over a long period of time or is it rather all of a sudden--the way some Amazon affiliate marketers do with paid reviews that glow? Not many reviews from said customers?

If you've seen the movie "Heat," with Al Pacino and Robert de Niro, you know when it is time to Walk Away. In the middle of a nighttime heist, Niro goes outside for a smoke. He hears a distant cough. Somewhere. Now, this is middle of the night in an unpopulated part of the city that comes from across the street - a parking lot full of what he thought were empty trailers. Hmm, he thinks maybe this isn't such a great night for a hot score. Not so empty (it was a cop in a trailer full of other hotshot cops). He walks back into the bank and tells his partner to abort.

The other aspect is time. Some fake sites will set a short ship time and count on you not bothering to see the sale as finalized before you can whistle Dixie out of your ass. After finalization, you're screwed since the money is in their wallet before you can even mount a protest.

Fraud Prevention

ONE IS Google believe it or not, at
http://www.google.com/imghp.

Dating sites like Cherry Blossoms and Cupid sometimes use reverse image search to catch fakers and Nigerian scammers masquerading as poor lonely singles to deprive men of their coinage. If they can catch them, so can you. If the image belongs to some other legit site, chances are it is fake. Foto Forensics also does the same, and reports metadata so that it becomes even harder to get away with Photoshop trickery.

When it is Okay to FE (Finalize Early)

FE MEANS 'FINALIZE EARLY'. It's use online can usually be found in black marketplaces like Silk Road and Sheep's Marketplace. It simply means that money in escrow is released before you receive your product. Every customer I've ever spoken with advises against this unless you've had great experience with that business.

But... quite a few vendors are now making it a *standard practice* to pay funds up front before you have anything in your hands.

On more than one Marketplace forum, there's been heated exchange as to when this is proper. You might hear, "Is this guy legit?

What about this Chinese outfit over here? He seems shady," and others: "A friend said this guy is okay but then I got ripped off!". You get the idea.

Here is my experience on the matter.

1.) It is okay when you are content with not getting what you paid for. This may seem counterproductive, but think how many gamblers go into a Las Vegas casino and never ask themselves "How much can I afford to lose?"

The answer, sadly, is not many. Vegas was not built on the backs of losers. Some merchants do not like escrow at all. Some do. So don't spend more than you can afford to lose. Look at it the way a gambler looks at making money.

2.) It is okay when you are guaranteed shipment. There are FE scammers out there that will give you an angelic smile and lie right into your eyes as they swindle you. Do not depend solely on reviews. A guy on SR can be the best merchant this side of Tatooine and yet you will wake up one day and find yourself robbed. He's split with a million in BTC and you're left not even holding a bag. Most won't do this to you. But a few will.

When it is NOT Okay to FE

WHEN LOSING your funds will result in you being evicted or a relationship severed. Never borrow money from friends and especially not family unless you want said family to come after you with a double-bladed ax. If you get ripped off, you lose not only the cash but the respect and trustworthiness of your family. Word spreads. You don't pay your debts. What's that saying in Game of Thrones?

Right. A Lannister always pays his debts. So should you.

MultiSigna

SOUNDS LIKE SOMETHING from Battlestar Galactica to pass from ship to ship. A badge of honor perhaps some hotshot flyboy wears on his fighter jacket that bypassed a lot of red tape.

While not exactly mandatory, it makes for interesting reading, and is something Tor users might want to know about if they wish to make purchases anonymously. Here's what happens:

When a purchase is enacted, the seller deposits money (in this case, Bitcoins) in a multi-signature address. After this, the customer gets notification to make the transaction ($,€) to the seller's account.

Then after the seller relays to MultiSigna that the transaction was a success, MultiSigna creates a transaction from the multi-signature address that requires both buyer and seller so that it may be sent to the network. The buyer gets the Bitcoins and ends the sale. Confused yet? I was too at first. You'll get used to it.

Critical

MULTISIGNA ONLY EXISTS AS A VERIFIER/COSIGNER of the entire transaction. If there is disagreement between seller and buyer, **no exchange** occurs. Remember the scene in Wargames when two nuclear silo operators have to turn their keys simultaneously in order to launch? Yeah, that.

MultiSigna will of course favor one or the other, but not both if they cannot mutually agree. The upside is that is if the market or purchaser or vendor loses a key, two out of three is still available. A single key cannot spend the money in 2/3 MultiSig address.

Is it Safe? Is it Secret?

I don't recommend enacting a million dollar exchange for a yacht, or even a thousand dollar one as they both carry risk, but ultimately it is up to you. Just remember that trust is always an issue on darknets, and you're generally safer making several transfers with a seller/buyer who has a good history of payment. In other words, reputation as always, is everything.

Alas, there are a few trustworthy markets that have good histories of doing things properly, thank heavens.

Blackbank is one. Agora is another. Take a look at the Multi-Sig Escrow Onion page here with Tor:

http://u5z75duioy7kpwun.onion/wiki/index.php/Multi-Sig_Escrow

Security

WHAT THE EFFECT would be if a hacker gained entry to the server? What mischief might he make? What chaos could he brew if he can mimic running a withdrawal in the same manner that the server does?

If a hacker were to gain access and attempt to withdraw money, a single-signature would be applied and passed to the second sig signer for co-signature. Then the security protocol would kick in where these policies would be enforced:

1.) Rate limits: the rate of stolen funds slows

2.) Callbacks to the spender's server: Signing service verifies with the original spender that they initiated and intended to make the spend. The callback could go to a separated machine, which could only contain access to isolated approved withdrawal information.

3.) IP limiting: The signing service only signs transactions coming from a certain list of IPs, preventing the case where the hacker or insider stole the private key.

4.) Destination Whitelists: Certain very high security wallets can be set such that the signing service would only accept if the destination were previously known. The hacker would have to compromise both the original sending server as well as the signing service.

Let me repeat that MultiSigna are *never in possession* of your bitcoins. They use 2 of 3 signatures (seller, buyer & MultiSigma) to sign a transaction. Normal transactions are signed by the seller and then by the buyer.

PURCHASER STEPS FOR MULTISIG ESCROW

1.) Deposit your Bitcoins. Purchase ability is granted after 6 confirmations

2.) Make a private & public key (Brainwallet.org is a JavaScript Client-Side Bitcoin Address Generator)

3.) Buy item, input public-key & a refund BTC address

4.) Retrieve purchased item

5.) Input the private key and close

TEN

THE LONG ARM OF THE LAW

Can the law steal funds?

Assuming you mean U.S. law, no, since the wallet does not contain the money. The Bitcoin blockchain prevents this. Hackers cannot steal it either since two private-keys are required and they will have had to steal 2 out of 3 private key holders... not likely.

WHAT ABOUT SAFETY in using the private key?

Never irresponsibly use the private key from your Bitcoin wallet. Create a new one instead. Give it the same love you give your True-crypt/DiskDecryptor master keys. Lots and lots of special love that no one else gets.

THIS SOUNDS AWFULLY RISKY. Won't I get caught?

Here is how most people get caught, and it really matters not what it is. Most dealers get busted making the usual mistakes:

- Bar Bragging

- Dropping too much personal data to strangers (I.e. Ross Ulbricht)
- Selling contraband to undercover law enforcement
- Snitches
- Committing crimes while under surveillance
- Managing an operation that grows by leaps and bounds (with loads of newbies making mistakes).

HOW FAR WILL the police go to catch you? That's a good question. The answer thought is pretty simple: As far as resources allow.

It'll probably be no worse than what Charleton Heston suffered being hogtied and dragged around the ape city, but know that some apes are worse than others.

It boils down to if what you're doing.

Case 1: In 2010, police in L.A. organized a phony sweepstakes scheme in order to lure in those with outstanding warrants. I kid you not, they did not come up with this idea themselves, but rather took it from The Simpsons.

They sent out close to a thousand fake letters under the name of a marketing group only to have a little over half a dozen show up at the La Mirada Inn for their free prize: A BMW 238. Nice, eh? Only the joke was on them as their smiles melted upon hearing those four dirty words, "You're all under arrest!"

The poor saps even brought ID to verify their identities. Dumb. They might as well have slapped on the cuffs themselves.

And this is an OFFLINE example. Imagine what one department can do by lying alone to an ISP or search engine. Threats of fines. Warrants. Bad publicity. Subpoenas of users. A bad reputation they are not likely to recover from soon. Police in Vegas in particular love to play dirty like this, dredging up old laws to ensure every member in that Ferbie operation has the book thrown at him.

IN 2013, a <u>Secret Service Agent</u> arrested several online by selling them fake IDs. The kicker?

They were all charged under the RICO Act of 1970. Originally created to put away mobsters, it allows them to lasso entire groups and charge each individual as if he committed the same crime everyone else in the group did... no matter the role.

Translation: The courier gets the same treatment as the ring-leader, as do the buyers. Individually, not much prison time in the grand scheme of things in 1970, but being charged as a GROUP? Twenty years minimum. Al Capone never saw such a hefty sentence.

It simply doesn't matter to a prosecutor if you're OS is encrypted and they can't get the data. All they need to prove is that you were part of the *enterprise* operation. That can be done outside of your shiny new Western Digital hard drive by subpoena to your ISP and a few other services you subscribe to. They've done this (and succeeded) with the newsgroup porn bust years ago in which every member of that hideous pedo group had encryption coming out of their ears.

Here was the short list of rules in that group.

- Never reveal true identity to another member of the group
- Never communicate with a member of the group outside usenet
- Group membership remains strictly within the confines of the Internet
- No member can positively identify another
- Members do not reveal personally identifying information
- Primary communications newsgroup is migrated regularly
- If a member breaks a security rule/fails to encrypt a message=BAN
- Periodically reduce chance of law enforcement discovery on each newsgroup migration by:
- Creating new PGP key pair, unlinking from previous messages
- Each member creates a new nickname
- Nickname theme selected by Yardbird (Group leader)

THE AFFIDAVITS READ like a Hell's Angels list of rules. And though I disagree with his (the website owner, not Yardbird) conclusion that "there are basically no nice people who provide case studies of OPSEC practices," I believe much can be learned by studying the habits of law-abiding citizen and criminal alike, especially considering the wide net over which the NSA is casting over *law abiding citizens.*

Remember that in Nazi Germany, if you slandered the SS, it was considered a capital offense. The film 'Sophie Scholl' is an excellent example of underground resistance movement for the right reason. It won accolades for its realistic portrayal of a college woman who stood up to the SS elite and was beheaded for it.

North Korea, Now. Same thing. They'd have little issues with doing worse. Beheading might be almost too lenient for them as they prefer prolonged, tortuous environments for their subjects. China? China has done some strange things, like outlawing stripping at funerals and banning Bitcoin transactions, and I do recall the violent protests by Muslims in 2010 and thinking "Those communist schmucks will round up all those screaming fools and shoot them at dawn and not look back!"

My Chinese girlfriend leaned over to me as we watched and mumbled, "They won't wait till dawn."

I like to think of Darkcoin as Bitcoin's smarter brother. Much smarter in fact, and darker. The best part of course being that it is constantly evolving.

Like Bitcoin they are a privacy-centric digital money based on the Bitcoin design. It's a design that allows for anonymity as you make day-to-day purchases on, well, just about anything so long as the digital store offers it.

With Bitcoin, anyone can see who made a purchase by only looking at the public blockchain. What Darkcoin does is anonymize your transaction *further* by using *Master nodes* - a decentralized network of servers that negate any requirement for third-parties: Parties that could scam you out of your coins.

Though few outlets use it, it is one of the quickest growing digital currencies out there, with an economy breaching over twenty million. Impressive. And that's not all. It's "Darksend" feature is quite fascinating--increasing privacy by compounding a typical transaction with *two* other users.

Needless to say, this is immensely attractive to a lot of Tor users who value high anonymity. Whistleblowers, journalists, underground political movements. That's the good list. The bad list though, well, you can never have the good without the bad: Terrorists. Contract killers. Tax evaders. Fallout players with the child-killing perk.

I hear the same arguments against its use that I heard with Freenet: Bad guys want to evade detection. Bad guys trade Darkcoins. You use Darkcoins. Therefore, you're a bad guy. Cue torches and pitchforks and black cats catapulted over the moat.

Heroin dealers love to use cash yet you never hear news outlets screaming about cash-only users linking to such a crime. Besides, the most corrupt money launderers are the central banks. It is *they* that allow states to borrow from future citizens to pay *today's* debts. One need only look at the National Debt to realize this.

But that's not to say Darkcoins are without issues. A few excellent questions have arisen:

- What if these "Masternodes" eventually form centralization?

- What if Darkcoin is abandoned by the creators once the price goes through the roof?

- Who is trustworthy enough to "audit" Darkcoin? We saw an audit with Truecrypt in 2013 which turned out to show no backdoors... except that the developers shut it down with a cryptic message saying Truecrypt was Not Secure Anymore. We can argue all day about what that meant.

These questions may never be answered. But that should not stop us from forging a new frontier in anonymity services.

Using Darkcoin for Business

IT IS much harder to run a Hidden Tor Service than it is to open a business using Darkcoin. It's so simple really that it boggles the mind what might be available in the future... and with minimal risk to you.

If this appeals to you, then get the Darkcoin Wallet. This is used to send/receive/store Darkcoin with the benefit of using Darksend for 100% anonymity. Most of your patrons will want you to have a wallet, so better to learn it early in the business rather than later.

Pick a Transaction Processor

BELOW ARE a few you can research to your liking. Not every processor will suit everyone just as every bank or credit union will not appeal to everyone. You must judge these yourself, weighing your needs with whatever risk your business entails. I've tried most of these and came away satisfied but like everything else with crypto currency, what works for me may not work for you.

ALTACCEPT
Fees
Transaction: 0.25% + 0.0005 DRK; Withdrawal: 0.01 DRK

COINPAYMENTS
Transaction: 0.50%; Withdrawal: Network transaction fee (TX)

COINTOPAY
Transactions: 0% (coin to coin) 0.5% (coin to fiat); Withdrawal: Network transaction fee (TX)
Transaction: 0.5%; Withdrawal: Included with transaction fee.

DARKCOIN   GRAPHICS   (COURTESY   of   the   Darkcoin
homepage)

After this you should signup to the Merchant Directory.

Then (optionally), do some reading on InstantX. InstantX is a double spend proof instant transaction method via the masternode network. Not exactly light reading, but the more you know...

NO SINGLE ENTITY has control of the entire system. Though the chance of an accident borders on the *not likely*, you need to remember that Darkcoin is still in development and because of that, unforeseen things happen. So a healthy dose of due diligence is required. I suggest only purchasing with money that doesn't break the bank in case bad luck happens upon you.

Frequent backups are mandatory for your wallet, more than Bitcoin since the anonymizing process executes more transactions in the background. If you've ever used Freenet, you know how slow the network can be and how much of a system resource hog anonymity often requires. Thus, make a new backup of your wallet whenever a you hit a coin ceiling.

ELEVEN

TOR HIDDEN SERVICES

How to Setup a Hidden Service on Tor

ONE BENEFIT to using Tor is that it allows you to create hidden services that will mask your identity to other users. In fact, you can have a website that is untraceable to you personally, provided you've taken all security precautions to keep your system updated. Here is an example of an onion site only accessible by using Tor:

HTTP://DUSKGYTLDKXIUQC6.ONION/

NATURALLY YOU CAN'T ACCESS this with your Firefox browser without Tor, hence the "hidden" name.

This chapter will give you the basics on what you need to set up your own Tor hidden service. It's not meant to be all-inclusive that covers everything and the kitchen sink, but only to give you an idea of the technical know-how you need to possess.

STEP ONE: Ensure Tor Works

Follow the directions on installing Tor, securing it against exploits and security vulnerabilities first and foremost.

Each OS has it's own vulnerabilities, with Windows being the worst. I recommend you go with Linux after you've mastered the basics as it gives you more control over Tor and is far more resistant to attacks than Windows.

Now might be a good time to state the obvious, something you've probably realized by now, and that is this: That no two counter-intelligence experts ever do the same thing the same way all the time. There is no red pill that makes it "All Clear." No cheat sheet of Magic Opsec Sauce that everyone can master if they only gulp it down. You can't memorize every organic compound combination in Organic Chemistry. Believe me, I tried. There were far too many.

What you do however is memorize the *general principles*, from which you can derive a solution to every problem that comes about. Anonymity is sometimes like that. Your strengths will not be your neighbor's strengths. Your weaknesses will be different as well. You adapt as you go along, and I can guarantee you your skills as a hobbyist will far exceed those working on the government dole.

STEP TWO: Installing Your Own Web Server

A local web server is the first thing you need to configure. It is a bit more involved than space here allows (without jacking the price).

You also want to keep this local server separate from any other installations that you have to avoid cross-contamination. In fact, you don't want ANY links between your hidden server and your day-to-day computer usage outside Tor.

Your server must be set to disallow any data leaks that might give away your identity. So you must attach the server to localhost only. If you're swapping trade secrets and don't want the boss to know, use a virtual machine to prevent DNS and other data leaks, but only if you can access the physical host yourself. Professional web hosting services (i.e. the Cloud) are a big no-no since it is stupid easy for the admin to snatch your encryption keys from RAM.

Go to http://localhost:8080/ via browser, since that is the port-number you entered at creation. Copy a text doc to the usual html-folder and ensure it copies successfully by logging into the webpage.

CONFIGURATION

Now comes the part where most people quit. Don't worry, it isn't hard. It's just that beginners see these numbers and think "Oh no... math!" and throw the book out the window.

But that's not what you'll do... because you're a *smart cookie.*

First, set your hidden-service to link to your own web-server. You can use Notepad to open your "torrc" file within Tor directory and do a search for the following piece of code:

########### This section is just for location-hidden services ###

As you can see, the hidden services function of Tor is edited out by the "#" sign, where each row relates to a hidden service. Hidden-ServiceDir is the section that will house all data about your own hidden service. Within this will be the hostname.file. This is where your onion-url will be.

The "HiddenServicePort" allows you to set a decoy port for redirects to throw off any efforts at detecting you. So add these to your torrc file.

HiddenServiceDir /Library/Tor/var/lib/tor/hidden_service/
HiddenServicePort 80 127.0.0.1:8080

Next, alter the HiddenServiceDir to the real directory from which Tor runs.

For Windows, use:

HiddenServiceDir
C:\Users\username\Documents\tor\hidden_service
HiddenServicePort 80 127.0.0.1:8080

FOR LINUX:

/home/username/hidden_service/, substituting "username" with whatever you named that directory.

RESTART TOR after saving the Torrc-file and it should be operational. Check your spelling if it throws out any errors.

Now then. Two files are created: the private_key and the hostname; private keys for your hidden service which you should keep under lock and key. The hostname is not your private key, however. You can give this to *anyone* you wish.

A descriptor for the hidden service links to other Tor servers and their respective directories so that Tor users can download it anonymously when they link or access to your hidden server.

OTHER POINTS of note

- Visitors to your hidden service may be able to identify whether your web-server is Thttpd or Apache.

- If your offline 50% of the time, so will your hidden service. Little bits (or lengthy ones, in this case) of data like this are useful to an adversary creating a profile on you.

- It is wiser to create a hidden service on Tor clients versus Tor relays as the relay uptime is visible to the public.

- Be aware that you are not a Node by default. On that point, it is advised to not have a relay running on the same machine as your hidden service as this opens security risks.

Shallot and Scallion Option

YOU ALSO HAVE the option of using Shallot or Scallion. Shallot allows one to create a customized .onion address for a hidden service, such as yyyyynewbietestyyyy.onion

On Running a Hidden Tor Server (and other Opsec Magic Sauce)

Having used Tor for many years, it came as a pleasant surprise to learn how few incidents there were in which the NSA managed to disrupt Tor. And I don't mean spam, either, but rather something that brought large sections of the network to a grinding halt. As it turns out, they're bark is much worse than their bite, especially if one is vigilant with their own secure setup.

The thing is, most Tor users couldn't be bothered. But then most users aren't interested in running a hidden server just as most P2P users don't bother seeding. Most are hit n' run downloaders. They know that as U.S. citizens they stand a good chance of getting sued if they leave their balls out there long enough. So some users opt to not further their own security knowledge. Let the Tor devs do it, they say. Can't be bothered.

Except most of the Tor advice by Tor developers I've read come up woefully inadequate. In fact I find that they aren't paranoid *nearly enough*. It's always been my belief that you can never be sufficiently paranoid as far as protecting your freedom is concerned, since the powers that be want to capture it and bottle it the way a cancer captures control of a cell: One organelle at a time with little of it's environment aware of the slow-boiling attack. To be honest... I suspect they *depend* on apathy and ignorance. And a lot of users gladly oblige.

Mr. Frog, meet boiling pot of water.

So then, what can we do? Well for starters, we can get the right security mindset.

TWELVE
TOR & YOUR RIG

Tor and Your PC

A secure computer is your best defense as the NSA mostly relies on man-in-the-middle attacks and browser exploits that deliver payloads to hidden Tor servers. That said, you should anticipate and expect such an exploit can infiltrate your system at any point. Things like Nits (network bugs), you have to be aware of. Thus the need to adhere to the following:

Use Linux whenever possible. Yes, I know you're comfortable using Windows and think Linux too much of a bother. But you won't if you're ISP is subpoenaed for something you said on Facebook. Something anti-feminist, for instance. So learn to use it.

The powers that be typically target the weakest system and the laziest users. The Tor Browser Bundle for Windows was instrumental in taking down Freedom Hosting and Silk Road because of unpatched vulnerabilities. That, and a few rogue Tor exit nodes patched unsigned Windows packages to spread malware.

If you're new to Linux, look at Linux Mint. If you're experienced, Debian is a good choice. Windows can't be trusted primarily because it is closed-source, but also because malware is more effective on it than Linux. If Linux is out of the question, consider Tails or Whonix as these apps come preconfigured to not allow any outgoing connections to clearnet.

Update Update Update

YOUR PC MUST ALSO BE UPDATED, ALWAYS. Not updating leads to vulnerabilities and exploits such as those in Windows. Optimally, you should ensure Tails is *always* updated each time you use Tor, and avoid any sites that use Java/Javascript/Flash or any kind of scripting as these execute code in ways you cannot see. Use these only in an emergency and never in your home system.

Avoid using cookies wherever possible. Consider installing the Self-Destructing Cookies add-on.

Again, you should not use anything but a portable PC since your home PC is most likely not portable enough to be discarded in a trash can in the event of compromise.

Avoid Google wherever possible. Use DuckDuckGo or Startpage instead for Tor sessions.

Situation Awareness

HERE WE GO AGAIN. But reading things three times often becomes a trigger in the brain later on for taking action, so here it is.

If an agency can monitor your local connection as well as the link you are browsing, then (with sufficient resources) they can apply traffic analysis to pinpoint your real location. Therefore, I recommend you do not use Tor in your residence.

Just to clarify, do not use Tor in your *legal* residence if doing any kind of covert work or anything *illegal* without strict security measures in place; the kind the average Tor user will likely overlook.

Let that other guy learn his lesson. It's a tough break, but better him than you. He's a 19 year old named Jimmy who likes hacking. You're a 32 year old construction guy with two kids and a mortgage. Who has more to lose? Right, you. So study counter-surveillance and counter-forensics like your life depends on it. Because it does!

For enemies of the state-level operations, I would suggest not engaging anything even near your online PC at home. Certainly nothing that makes you think you need Tor to hide it. It may be fine for private browsing but not for someone planning a coup, running an illegal operation (home bible study in Iran, for instance), or trying to disappear.

Be wary of using it in hotels as well, where often there are many cams watching with 24/hr surveillance. That location can be linked to Tor activity.

Do not use Tor more than a day in any specific location. A correlation-attack can be done in less than an hour if a black van is parked nearby--a van you will not see. They may not slap the cuffs on you as you walk out of the cafe that very week, but later they might. Consider the area a toxic dump after a day, regardless if you must travel to the next shop or town.

If you want to get really cloak and dagger about it, have an app running (an MMO, for instance) while you are out and about doing your Tor activity that makes it look like you were home during that time.

THIRTEEN

TOR HIDDEN SERVICES RULES

High Risk, High Reward

CNN, along with FoxNews and a hotbed of other media outlets, has been trumpeting the defeat of certain hidden services for a few years now. It makes for good headlines. Services like Silk Road and Freedom Hosting, which I'm sure you've heard about. They are a easy target for the FBI since hidden services are not high on the list of priorities by Tor developers yet. Same for the NSA.

Both agencies know every trick and hack there is to know about running a hidden service. And so should you. This is not to say you need the expertise to match their team of super hackers, but that you need even more vigilance to run such a service than you do *visiting* such a service.

Priority number one is simple: if you run one, you must own one. They must not be run under somebody else's control if you can help it, because if that service is compromised, *everyone* goes down. That means total anonymity, 100% of the time with world-class jewel-thief stealth ability.

The Silk Road admin did not have this ability. In fact, looking through the online docs detailing the arrest, one gets the impression he was very lax in IT security procedure. He repeatedly made mistakes such that luck on the part of LE never really came into it at all. The guy was just sloppy.

FIRST

Never, ever, ever run a hidden service within a VM that is owned by a friend or a Cloud space provider. Remember, all "The Cloud" is, is someone *else's* drive or network, not your own. Encryption keys can be dumped from RAM. And who owns the RAM?

Right. The Cloud provider. Lightning strikes and there goes your own anonymity as well as the anonymity of your visitors if they are lazy in their browser habits. The FBI delivered a "nit" (network investigative technique) this way to unpatched Tor Browser Bundles in 2013. If, however, you own the machine, then it's a different story. But let's back up a few steps and assume you don't. How might you go about running it on a host system?

Well first off, you would need two separate physical hosts from different parties, both running in virtual machines with a firewall-enabled OS that only allows Tor network activity and *nothing else.*

The second physical host is the one the hidden service runs from, also VM'ed. Secure connections are enabled by IPSec. What's IPSec, you ask?

"IPSec is a protocol suite, for securing Internet Protocol (IP) communications by authenticating and encrypting each IP packet of a communication session. IPsec can be used in protecting data flows between a pair of hosts (host-to-host), between a pair of security gateways (network-to-network), or between a security gateway and a host (network-to-host)."

If an intruder agent tampers with anything, you will know about it and can shut down the service or move it to a safer place, and all while being a ghost in the machine. You can imagine how valuable this would be in North Korea.

If you were in that cesspool of a country, you would be more than a little paranoid if the server went down even for a few seconds. But you could always move it to a more secure location or even start over, and you might just want to since you would not know if a RAID failure had occurred or if some commie jackboot was sending a copy of the VM to the higher ups.

SECOND

If going the host route, you must ensure that remote-console is always available to you by the host, any time you want. You must do everything remotely, in fact, and change passwords frequently via https. I'd say once per day as paranoia in such a climate as North Korea would be good for your health.

THIRD

You must never, not even once, access the service from home. Not from your Nexus 7. Not from your girlfriend's Galaxy Note. Not even via Tor from your backyard using your neighbor's WiFi. Using a VPN as well is risky unless you know what you're doing. Only access it via secure locations at least ten miles away from your residence. Overkill, some might say, but then there is no such thing as overkill in a gulag.

FOURTH

Move the service on occasion. Again, look at any Youtube video on how snipers train to take out an enemy. They move place to place after each shot to conceal the true location from the enemy. How often is up to you. Once a week? Once a month? Personally I'd say every twenty-one days. You can never be too secure when running one of these.

FOURTEEN

DARKNET PERSONAS

"We've been watching you Mr. Anderson, and it seems you've been living... two lives. One of them has a future, and one does not." -- Agent Smith, The Matrix

YOU'VE no doubt read of Tor busts where an undercover agent snagged a phone number or clearnet nic from someone they were targeting because said target trusted too much, too quickly. Take it from Yoda - You can avoid this by retraining yourself, *unlearning* what you've learned.

You must consider your Tor sessions the property of your other

Self. The cloned You - that shadowy thievish looking guy above. The *second* You. One that despises Incubus and loves Tool and views Neo as just another beta-orbiting punk who got the luck of the draw when Morpheus and crew unplugged him. This clone would not use Twitter or YouTube or other social gunk. He would never hang with you nor call you up for a few beers. In fact, he hates beer, preferring J&B as he hacks with John Carpenter's The Thing OST playing as mood music in the background. That's your other *You*. The smarter you.

And he must be the new You *on Tor*. And you must forever separate him from the non-Tor You.

His Facebook, Twitter and YouTube accounts are all fake, having never once used them on his home PC.

His nics are different, as is his passwords, likes/dislikes and even the fonts he uses to browse the Deep Web. Mixing this dark persona with your own would be like the boy made of matter kissing the antimatter girl.

Boom.

Further, any phone calls this person makes is done by prepaid phones that were not purchased by any credit cards he holds. He is a cash n' carry guy and then only if he is twenty miles from home. Any *SIM* cards he uses are strictly used in conjunction with Tor activity and never used in phones the *other guy* uses. And... he deliberately leaves false info wherever he goes. Kinda like the CIA does.

But to better clarify this idea, let's assume John Doe doesn't know any better. He watches a movie on Netflix. Then he mosies on over to Freenet and drops intel without even realizing it, eager to share his great cinema experience with his darknet buds (no pun).

"Hey guys, just watched a cool flick with Russell Crowe. Kinda Michael Bay-ish and Liam Neeson's cameo was too short, but makes for a good flick if you want to learn how to disappear. But those police, sweet Jesus! Those rent-a-cop guys sure are as dumb as a sack of bricks!"

Police are dumb, he says.

Metadata is collected by Netflix just as it is with Google and Yahoo. Every single user. They know every film you viewed and even which ones you hated. He's even made forum posts indicating similar weather and, though not mentioning names, has griped about local politicians being handcuffed in very geo-specific arrests, even dropping the charges!

How many Netflix fans do you think watched this movie at the time of his Freenet post? How many in cities that had local politicians arrested for embezzling? How many with similar weather depicted in the film? Most likely less than ten. Maybe not even that.

There is also the handwriting element. Does he *mispell* the same words over and over? Throw commas like daggers? Misuse semi-colons and run-on sentences? System clock out of sync with his posts? All of this leads to a great profile that ties his IP address to his identity. Often it is enough to get a warrant if he so much as whispers that he's obtained any kind of contraband.

Unless of course, all of this info is tailor-made to fit the other *You*.

We already know that the VPN called Hide-My-Ass as well as Hushmail and Lavabit stabbed their users in the back when threats by a judge became too heated ($5000 a day in Lavabit's case, until they forked over user data). And all this just so they could track Edward Snowden.

Bottom line: Learn from Snowden's mistakes. Take every company's claim of anonymity with a grain of salt. The proof is in the amount of arrests tied to said company or app. In the case of Freenet, none.

But there is always a first time. Recall that they only have to get lucky once, which more often than not relies on your carelessness.